"How readest thou?"

"HOW READEST THOU?"

J.C. RYLE

CHARLES NOLAN PUBLISHERS
MOSCOW

First published in 1852
First Charles Nolan Publishers edition 2002
© 2002 by Charles Nolan Publishers
All rights reserved. Published 2002
Printed in the United States of America
This book is printed on acid-free paper.
ISBN 0-9677603-3-X

Explanatory footnotes have been supplied by the publisher.

CHARLES NOLAN PUBLISHERS
MOSCOW, IDAHO
UNITED STATES of AMERICA

CONTENTS

1. Knowledge of Biblical Truth is Needful for Salvation   7

2. No Book is Written in Such a Manner as the Bible   10

3. No Book Contains Such Important Matter as the Bible   16

4. No Book Has Done So Much *for* the World as the Bible   22

5. No Book Can Do So Much as the Bible   28

6. No Book Has Been so Neglected & Misused as the Bible   33

7. The Bible is the Only Rule   39

8. All True Servants of God Love the Bible   43

9. Only the Bible Can Comfort a Dying Man   48

10. Conclusion   53

What is written in the law? How readest thou?
                                    LUKE 10:26

READER,

The question before your eyes is 1800 years old. It was asked by our Lord Jesus Christ. It was asked concerning the Bible.

I invite you to examine and consider this question. I warn you, it is just as mighty and important now as it was on the day when it came from our Lord's lips. I want to apply it to the conscience of every one who reads this paper, and to knock at the door of his heart. I would fain sound a trumpet in the ear of every one who speaks English, and cry aloud, "How readest thou? Dost thou read the Bible?"

Why do I hold this question to be of such mighty importance? Why do I press it on the notice of every man, as a matter of life and death? Give me your attention for a few minutes, and you shall see. Follow me through these pages, and you shall hear why I ask, "How READEST THOU? DOST THOU READ THE BIBLE?"

1. Knowledge of Biblical Truth is Needful for Salvation

I ask, first of all, because *there is no knowledge absolutely needful to a man's salvation, except a knowledge of the things which are to be found in the Bible.*

We live in days when the words of Daniel are fulfilled before our eyes: "Many run to and fro, and knowledge is increased." (Dan. 12:4.) Schools are multiplying on every side. New colleges are set up. Old universities are reformed and improved. New books are continually coming forth. More is being taught, more is being learned, more is being read, than there ever was since the world began. It is all well. I rejoice at it. An ignorant population is a perilous and expensive burden to any nation. It is a ready prey to the first Absalom, or Catiline, or Wat Tyler, or Jack Cade, who may arise to entice it to do evil.[1] But this I say—we must never forget that all the education a man's head can receive will not save his soul from hell, unless he knows the truths of the Bible.

A man *may have prodigious learning, and yet never be saved.* He may be master of half the languages spoken round the globe. He may be acquainted with the highest and deepest things in heaven and earth. He may have read books till he is like a walking cyclopædia. He may be familiar with the stars of heaven, the birds of the air, the beasts of the earth, and the fishes of the sea. He may be able, like Solomon, to "speak of trees, from the cedar of Lebanon to the hyssop that grows on the wall, of beasts also, and fowls, and creeping things, and fishes." (1 Kings 4:33.) He may be able to discourse of all the secrets of fire, air, earth, and water. And yet, if he dies ignorant of Bible truths, he dies a miserable man. Chemistry never silenced a guilty conscience. Mathematics never healed a broken heart. All the sciences in the world never smoothed down a dying pillow. No earthly philosophy ever supplied hope in death. No natural theology ever gave peace in the prospect of meeting a holy God. All these things are of the earth, earthy, and can never raise a man above the earth's level. They may enable a man to strut and fret his little season here below with a more dignified gait than his fellow mortals, but they can never give him wings, and enable him to soar towards heaven. He that has the largest share of them will find at length that without Bible knowledge he has got no lasting possession. Death will make an end of all his attainments, and after death they will do him no good at all.

A man *may be a very ignorant man, and yet be saved.* He may be unable to read a word, or write a letter. He may know nothing

---

[1] All four men led failed rebellions against their respective governments: Absalom rebelled against his father, King David (2 Sam. 15—18); Catiline (*d.* 62 B.C.) against the late Roman Republic; Wat Tyler (*d.* 1381) against Richard II; and Jack Cade (*d.* 1450) against Henry VI.

of geography beyond the bounds of his own parish, and be utterly unable to say which is nearest, Paris or New York. He may know nothing of arithmetic, and not see any difference between a million and a thousand. He may know nothing of history, not even of his own land, and be quite ignorant whether his country owes most to Semiramis, Boadicea, or Queen Elizabeth.[1] He may know nothing of the affairs of his own times, and be incapable of telling you whether the Chancellor of the Exchequer, or the Commander-in-Chief, or the Archbishop of Canterbury is managing the national finances. He may know nothing of science and its discoveries: and whether Julius Cæsar won his victories by gunpowder, or the apostles had a printing press, or the Sun goes round the Earth, may be matters about which he has not an idea. And yet if that very man has heard Bible truth with his ears, and believed it with his heart, he knows enough to save his soul. He will be found at last with Lazarus in Abraham's bosom,[2] while his scientific fellow-creature, who has died unconverted, is lost for ever.

Knowledge of the Bible, in short, is the one knowledge that is needful. A man may get to heaven without money, learning, health, or friends—but without Bible knowledge he will never get there at all. A man may have the mightiest of minds, and a memory stored with all that mighty mind can grasp—and yet, if he does not know the things of the Bible, he will make shipwreck of his soul for ever. Woe! woe! woe to the man who dies in ignorance of the Bible!

Reader, this is the book about which I am addressing you today. It is no light matter *what you do with such a book*. It concerns the life of your soul. I summon you—I charge you to give an honest answer to my question. What art thou doing with the Bible? Dost thou read it? How READEST THOU?

---

[1] Semiramis was a legendary ninth-century B.C. Assyrian queen; Boadicea was a British queen who died in A.D. 60; and Queen Elizabeth (1533–1603) was the first Protestant Queen of England.

[2] Prior to the Lord Jesus' death, Scripture divided the "state after death" into two places: one for the righteous and one for the wicked. In the Parable of the Rich Man & Lazarus (Luke 16:19–31), the phrase "Abraham's bosom" denotes the place where the righteous, those who died in faith, waited for their redemption.

2. No Book is Written in Such a Manner as the Bible

I ask, in the second place, because *there is no book in existence written in such a manner as the Bible.*

The Bible is "given by inspiration of God." (2 Tim. 3:16.) In this respect it is utterly unlike all other writings. God taught the writers of it what to say. God put into their minds thoughts and ideas. God guided their pens in setting down those thoughts and ideas. When you read it, you are not reading the self-taught compositions of poor imperfect men like yourself, but the words of the eternal God. When you hear it, you are not listening to the erring opinions of short-lived mortals, but to the unchanging mind of the King of kings. The men who were employed to indite the Bible "spake not of themselves." They "spake as they were moved by the Holy Ghost." (2 Pet. 1:21.) All other books in the world, however good and useful in their way, are more or less defective. The more you look at them, the more you see their defects and blemishes. The Bible alone is absolutely perfect. From beginning to end it is "the Word of God."

I shall not waste time by attempting any long and laboured proof of this. I say boldly that the book itself is the best witness of its own inspiration. It is utterly inexplicable and unaccountable in any other point of view. It is the greatest standing miracle in the world. He that dares to say the Bible is not inspired, let him give a reasonable account of it, if he can. Let him explain the history and character of the book in a way that will satisfy any man of common sense. The burden of proof seems to my mind to lie on him. I shall content myself with stating some plain facts about the Bible, which can neither be denied nor explained away. And the ground I shall take up is this, that these facts ought to satisfy every reasonable inquirer that the Bible is of God, and not of man. They are simple facts, which require no knowledge of Hebrew, or Greek, or Latin, in order to be understood; yet they are facts which prove to my own mind conclusively that the Bible is superhuman, or not of man.

(*a*) It is a fact that there is an *extraordinary unity and harmony in the contents of the Bible*, which is entirely above man. We all know how difficult it is to get a story told by any three persons, not living together, in which there are not some contradictions and discrepancies. If the story is a long one, and involves a large quantity of particulars, unity seems almost impossible among the common run of men. But it is not so with the Bible. Here is a book written by not less than thirty different persons. The writers were men of every rank and class in society. One was a lawgiver. One was a warlike king. One was a peaceful king. One was a herdsman. One had been brought up as a publican, another as a physician, another as a learned Pharisee, two as fishermen, several as priests. They lived at different intervals, over a space of 1500 years; and the greater part of them never saw each other face to face. And yet there is a perfect harmony among all these writers. They all write as if they were under one dictation. The handwriting may vary, but the mind that runs through their work is always one and the same. They all tell the same story. They all give one account of man, one account of God, one account of the way of salvation, one account of the heart. You see truth unfolding under their hands, as you go through the volume of their writings—but you never detect any real contradiction, or contrariety of view.

I ask my readers to mark this fact, and ponder it well. Tell me not that this unity might be the result of chance. The man who can believe *that* must indeed be a credulous person. There is only one satisfactory account of the book. The Bible is not of man, but of God. *It was written under the direct inspiration of God.*

(b) It is another fact that there is an *extraordinary accuracy in the facts and statements of the Bible, which is above man.* Here is a book that has been finished and before the world for more than 1800 years. These 1800 years have been the busiest and most changeful period the world has ever seen. During this period the greatest discoveries have been made in science, the greatest alterations in the ways and customs of society, the greatest improvements in the habits and usages of life. Hundreds of things might be named which satisfied and pleased our forefathers, which we have laid aside long ago as obsolete, useless, and old-fashioned. The laws, the books, the houses, the furniture, the clothes, the carriages of each succeeding century, have been a continual improvement on those of the century that went before. There is hardly a work of brain or hands in which faults and weak points have not been discovered. There is hardly an institution which has not gone through a process of sifting, purifying, refining, simplifying, reforming, amending, and changing. But all this time men have never discovered a weak point or a defect in the Bible. Infidels have assailed it in vain. There it stands—perfect, and fresh, and complete—as it did eighteen centuries ago. The march of intellect never overtakes it. The wisdom of wise men never gets beyond it. The science of philosophers never proves it wrong. The discoveries of travellers never convict it of mistakes. Are the distant islands of the Pacific laid open? Nothing is found that in the slightest degree contradicts the Bible account of man's heart. Are the ruins of Nineveh and Egypt ransacked and explored? Nothing is found that overturns one jot or tittle of the Bible's historical statements. On the contrary, they are continually receiving fresh confirmation. How shall we account for this fact? Who could have thought it possible that so large a book, handling such a vast variety of subjects, should, at the end of these years, be found so free from erroneous statements? There is only one satisfactory account to be given of the fact. The Bible was written by inspiration of God.

(c) It is another fact that there is an *extraordinary wisdom, sublimity, and majesty in the style of the Bible,* which is above man. Strange and unlikely as it was, the writers of Scripture have produced a book which even at this day is utterly unrivalled. With all our boasted attainments in science and art and learning, we can produce nothing in literature that can be compared with the Bible. Even at this very hour, in the nineteenth century, the book stands entirely alone. No other book in existence comes near it. There is a strain and a style and a tone of thought about it, which separate it from all other writings. There are no weak points, and motes, and flaws, and blemishes. There is no mixture of infirmity and feebleness, such as you will find in the works of even the best Christians. "Holy, holy, holy," seems written on every page. (Isa. 6:3; Rev. 4:8.) To talk of comparing the Bible with other "sacred books" so-called, such as the Koran, the Shasters, or the Book of Mormon, is positively absurd. You might as well compare the Sun with a rushlight, or Mount Blanc with a molehill, or St. Paul's with an Irish hovel, or the Portland Vase with a garden pot, or the Koh-i-noor diamond with a bit of glass.[1]

[1] Mount Blanc is the highest peak in the Alps (15,771 feet); St. Paul's Cathedral, London, is a universally known landmark of the City; the Port-

God seems to have allowed the existence of these pretended revelations in order to prove the immeasurable superiority of His own Word. To talk of the inspiration of the Bible as only differing *in degree* from that of such writings as the works of Homer, Plato, Shakespeare, Danté, and Milton is simply a piece of blasphemous folly. Every honest and unprejudiced reader must see that there is a gulf between the Bible and any other book, which no man can fathom. You feel at turning from the Scriptures to other works that you have got into a new atmosphere. You feel like one who has exchanged gold for base metal, and heaven for earth. And how can this mighty difference be accounted for? The men who wrote the Bible had no special advantages. They lived in a remote corner of the civilized earth. They had, most of them, little leisure, few books, and no learning—such as learning is reckoned in this world. Yet the book they composed is one which is unrivalled! There is but one way of accounting for this fact. *They wrote under the direct inspiration of God.*

(*d*) It is another fact that there is in the Bible an extraordinary *suitableness to the spiritual wants of all mankind.* It exactly meets the heart of man in every rank or class, in every country and climate, in every age and period of life. It is the only book in existence which is never out of place and out of date. Other books after a time become obsolete and old-fashioned. The Bible never does. Other books suit one country or people, and not another. The Bible suits all. It is the book of the poor and unlearned, no less than of the rich and the philosopher. It feeds the mind of the labourer in his cottage, and it satisfies the gigantic intellects of Chalmers, Brewster, and Faraday.[1] Lord Macaulay, and John Bright,[2] and the writers of brilliant articles in the *Times*, and the humblest city missionaries are all under obligations to the same volume. It is equally valued by the converted New Zealander in

---

land Vase is a first-century A.D. vase considered the finest surviving Roman example of cameo glass; and the Koh-i-noor (Persian, "Mountain *of* Light") diamond is a magnificent stone, weighing 109 carats, placed among the crown jewels of Queen Victoria.

[1] Thomas Chalmers (1780–1847), Sir David Brewster (1781–1868), and Michael Faraday (1791–1867) were scientific geniuses who submitted their minds to the Scriptures.

[2] Thomas Macaulay (1800–1859) and John Bright (1811–1889) were British political reformers known for their evangelical faith.

the southern hemisphere, and the Red River Indian in the cold north of America, and the Hindoo under the tropical sun.

It is the only book, moreover, which seems always fresh and ever green and new. For eighteen centuries it has been studied and prayed over by millions of private Christians, and expounded and explained and preached to us by thousands of ministers. Fathers, and schoolmen, and Reformers, and Puritans, and modern divines have incessantly dug down into the mine of Scripture, and yet never exhausted it. It is a well never dry, and a field which is never barren. It meets the hearts and minds and consciences of Christians in the nineteenth century as fully as it did those of Greeks and Romans when it was first completed. It suits the "dairyman's daughter" as well as Persis, or Tryphena, or Tryphosa[1]—and the English peer as well as the converted African at Sierra Leone. It is still the first book which fits the child's mind when he begins to learn religion, and the last to which the old man clings as he leaves the world. In short, it suits all ages, ranks, climates, minds, conditions. It is the one book which suits the world.

Now how shall we account for this singular fact? What satisfactory explanation can we give? There is only one account and explanation. The Bible was *written by divine inspiration.* It is the book of the world, because He inspired it who formed the world, who made all nations of one blood, and knows man's common nature. It is the book for every heart, because He dictated it who alone knows all hearts, and what all hearts require. *It is the Book of God.*

It proves nothing against inspiration, as some have asserted, that the writers of the Bible have each a different style. Isaiah does not write like Jeremiah, and Paul does not write like John. This is perfectly true—and yet the works of these men are not a whit less equally inspired. The waters of the sea have many different shades. In one place they look blue, and in another green. And yet the difference is owing to the depth or shallowness

---

[1] *The Dairyman's Daughter* is the title of a nineteenth-century bestseller by Legh Richmond (1772–1827), which tells the extraordinary life, conversion, and untimely death of a very ordinary Welsh maid, Elizabeth Wallbridge (1770–1801). Persis, Tryphena, and Tryphosa are three women named in Scripture of whom we only know that they served the Lord Jesus Christ. (Rom. 16:12.)

of the part we see, or to the nature of the bottom. The water in every case is the same salt sea. The breath of a man may produce different sounds, according to the character of the instrument on which he plays. The flute, the pipe, and the trumpet have each their peculiar note. And yet the breath that calls forth the notes is in each case one and the same. The light of the planets we see in heaven is very various. Mars, and Saturn, and Jupiter have each a peculiar colour. And yet we know that the light of the Sun, which each planet reflects, is in each case one and the same. Just in the same way, the books of the Old and New Testaments are all inspired truth, and yet the aspect of that truth varies according to the mind through which the Holy Ghost makes it flow. The handwriting and style of the writers differ enough to prove that each had a distinct individual being; but the Divine Guide who dictates and directs the whole is always one. All is alike inspired. *Every chapter, and verse, and word is from God.*

Set down this fact in your mind, and do not forget it. The extraordinary contents of the Bible are a great fact which can only be explained by admitting its inspiration. Let my reader mark well what I say. It is a simple broad fact that in the matter of *contents*, the Bible stands entirely alone, and no other book is fit to be named in the same day with it.

Oh! that men who are troubled with doubts, and questionings, and sceptical thoughts about inspiration would calmly examine the Bible for themselves! Oh! that they would act on the advice which was the first step to Augustine's conversion—"Take it up and read it!—take it up and read it!"[1] How many Gordian knots[2] this course of action would cut! How many difficulties and objections would vanish away at once, like mist before the rising Sun! How many would soon confess, "The finger of God is here! God is in this book, and I knew it not."

---

[1] Augustine of Hippo (354–430), esteemed theologian of the Latin Fathers; Romans 13:13–14 led to his conversion.

[2] When Alexander the Great (356–323 B.C.) marched through Gordium in 333 B.C., he saw the chariot of the city's founder, Gordius, with its yoke lashed to a pole by means of an intricate knot with its end hidden. According to tradition, this knot could only be untied by the future conqueror of Asia. Legend says that Alexander sliced through the knot with his sword. The proverbial phrase "cut the Gordian knot" has thus come to denote a bold solution to a complicated problem.

Reader, this is the book about which I address you this day. Surely it is no light matter *what you are doing with this Book*. It is no light thing that God should have caused this book to be "written for your learning," and that you should have before you "the oracles of God." (Rom. 15:4; 3:2.) I charge you, I summon you to give an honest answer to my question. What art thou doing with the Bible? Dost thou read it at all? How READEST THOU?

3. No Book Contains Such Important Matter as the Bible

I ask, in the third place, because *no book in existence contains such important matter as the Bible*.

There is an *extraordinary depth, fulness, and richness in the contents of the Bible*. It throws more light on a vast number of most important subjects than all the other books in the world put together. It boldly handles matters which are utterly beyond the reach of man, when left to himself. It treats of things which are mysterious and invisible—the soul, the world to come, and eternity—depths which man has no line to fathom. All who have tried to write of these things, without Bible light, have done little but show their own ignorance. They grope like the blind; they speculate; they guess; they generally make the darkness more visible, and land us in a region of uncertainty and doubt. How little did the wisest of the heathen know! How dim were the views of Socrates, Plato, Cicero, and Seneca! A well-taught Sunday-school child, in the present day, knows more spiritual truth than all these sages put together.

The Bible alone gives a reasonable account of *the beginning and end of the globe on which we live*. It starts from the birthday of the Sun, Moon, stars, and Earth in their present order, and shows us creation in its cradle. It foretells minutely the dissolution of all things—when the stars shall fall from their places, and the Earth and all its works shall be burned up—and shows us creation in its grave. It tells us the story of the world's youth, and it tells us the story of its old age. It gives us the picture of its first days, and it gives us the picture of its last. How vast and important is this knowledge!

The Bible alone gives *a true and faithful account of man*. It does not flatter him as novels and romances do. It does not conceal his faults and exaggerate his goodness. It paints him just as he is. It describes him as a fallen creature, very far gone from original righteousness, and of his own nature inclined to evil—a creature needing not only a pardon, but a new heart, to make him fit for heaven. It shows him to be a corrupt being, under every possible circumstance, when left to himself—corrupt after the loss of Paradise, corrupt after the Flood, corrupt when fenced in by laws and commandments, corrupt when the Son of God visited him as manifest in the flesh, corrupt in the face of warnings, corrupt in the face of miracles, corrupt in the face of judgments, corrupt in the face of mercies. In one word—it shows man to be by nature always a sinner. How important is this knowledge!

The Bible alone gives us *true views of God*. By nature man knows nothing of Him. All his conceptions and ideas of Him are low, grovelling, and debased. What could be more degraded than the gods of the Canaanites and Egyptians—of Babylon, of Greece, and of Rome? What can be more vile than the gods of the Hindoos, and other heathens, in our own times? By the Bible we know that *God hates sin*. The destruction of the world by the Flood, the burning of Sodom and Gomorrah, the drowning of Pharaoh and the Egyptians in the Red Sea, the cutting off of the nations of Canaan, the overthrow of Jerusalem and the temple, the scattering of the Jews—all these are unmistakable witnesses.[1] By the Bible we know that *God loves sinners*. His gracious promise in the day of Adam's fall; His longsuffering in the times of Noah; His deliverance of Israel out of the land of Egypt; His gift of the law at Mount Sinai; His bringing the tribes into the promised land; His forbearance in the days of the Judges and Kings; His repeated warnings by the mouth of His prophets; His restoration of Israel after the Babylonian captivity; His sending His Son into the world, in due time, to be crucified; His commanding the gospel to be preached to the Gentiles—all these are speaking facts. By the Bible we learn that *God knows all things*. We see Him foretelling things hundreds and thousands of years before they take place: and as He foretells, so it comes to pass. He foretold that the family of Ham should be a servant of servants, that Tyre

---

[1] See Gen. 6:17; 19:24–28; Exod. 15:27, 28; Deut. 19:1; Josh. 23:4; Rom. 11:25.

should become a rock for drying nets, that Nineveh should become a desolation, that Babylon should be made a desert, that Egypt should be the basest of kingdoms, that Edom should be forsaken and uninhabited, and that the Jews should not be reckoned among the nations.[1] All these things were utterly unlikely and improbable. Yet all have been fulfilled. Reader, once more I say, how vast and important is all this knowledge!

The Bible alone teaches us that *God has made a full, perfect, and complete provision for the salvation of fallen man.* It tells of an atonement made for the sin of the world, by the sacrifice and death of God's own Son upon the cross. It tells us that by His death for sinners, as their substitute, He has obtained eternal redemption for all that believe on Him. The claims of God's broken law have now been satisfied. "Christ has suffered for sin, the just for the unjust." (1 Pet. 3:18.) God can now be just, and yet the justifier of the ungodly. It tells us that there is now a complete remedy for the guilt of sin—even the precious blood of Christ—and peace and rest of conscience for all who believe on Christ. "Whosoever believeth on Him shall not perish, but have eternal life." (John 3:15.) It tells us that there is a complete remedy for the power of sin—even the almighty grace of the Spirit of Christ. It shows us the Holy Ghost quickening believers, and making them new creatures. It promises a new heart and a new nature to all who will hear Christ's voice and follow Him. Reader, once more I say, how important is this knowledge!

The Bible alone *explains the state of things that we see in the world around us.* There are many things on Earth which a natural man cannot explain. The amazing inequality of conditions, the poverty and distress, the oppression and persecution, the shakings and tumults, the failures of statesmen and legislators, the constant existence of uncured evils and abuses—all these things are often puzzling to him. He sees, but does not understand. But the Bible makes it all clear. The Bible can tell him that man is a fallen creature, and is of his own nature inclined to evil; that the whole world lieth in wickedness; that the prince of the world, the devil, is everywhere; and that it is vain to look for perfection in the present order of things. The Bible will tell him that neither laws

---

[1] See Gen. 9:25; Ezek. 26:1–21; Zeph. 2:13; Isa. 13:19–22; Ezek. 29:1–16; Jer. 49:7–22; Deut. 28:63–65.

nor education can ever change men's hearts; and that just as no man will ever make a machine work well, unless he allows for friction, so also no man will do much good in the world, unless he always remembers that human nature is fallen, and that the world he works in is full of sin. The Bible will tell him that there is "a good time"[1] certainly coming—and coming perhaps sooner than people expect it—a time of perfect knowledge, perfect justice, perfect happiness, and perfect peace. But the Bible will tell him this time shall not be brought in by any power but that of Christ coming to Earth again. And for that second coming of Christ, the Bible will tell him to prepare. Oh! reader, how important is all this knowledge!

But time would fail me, if I were to enter fully into all the great things which the Bible reveals. It is not by any sketch or outline that the treasures of the Bible can be displayed. It would be easy to point out many other things, beside those I have mentioned, and yet the half of its riches would be left untold.

How comforting is the account it gives us of the great Mediator of the New Testament—the man Christ Jesus! Four times over His picture is graciously drawn before our eyes. Four separate witnesses tell us of His miracles and His ministry; His sayings and His doings; His life and His death; His power and His love; His kindness and His patience; His ways, His words, His works, His thoughts, His heart. Blessed be God, there is one thing in the Bible the most prejudiced reader can hardly fail to understand, and that is the character of Jesus Christ!

How encouraging are the examples the Bible gives us of good people! It tells us of many who were of like passions with ourselves—men and women who had cares, crosses, families, temptations, afflictions, diseases, like ourselves—and yet "by faith and patience inherited the promises," and got safe home. (Heb. 6:12.) It keeps back nothing in the history of these people. Their mistakes, their infirmities, their conflicts, their experience, their prayers, their praises, their useful lives, their happy deaths—all are fully recorded. And it tells us the God and Saviour of these men and women still waits to be gracious, and is altogether unchanged.

[1] Quoted from "The Good Time Coming" (1846), a popular nineteenth-century song written by Charles Mackay (1814–1889).

How instructive are the examples the Bible gives us of bad people! It tells us of men and women who had light, and knowledge, and opportunities, like ourselves, and yet hardened their hearts, loved the world, clung to their sins, would have their own way, despised reproof, and ruined their own souls for ever. And it warns that the God who punished Pharaoh, and Saul, and Ahab, and Jezebel, and Judas, and Ananias and Sapphira, is a God who never alters, and that there is a hell.[1]

How precious are the promises which the Bible contains for the use of those who love God! There is hardly any possible emergency or condition for which it has not some "word in season." (Isa. 50:4.) And it tells men that God loves to be put in remembrance of these promises, and that if He has said He will do a thing, His promise shall certainly be performed.

How blessed are the hopes which the Bible holds out to the believer in Christ Jesus! Peace in the hour of death, rest and happiness on the other side of the grave, a glorious body in the morning of the resurrection, a full and triumphant acquittal in the day of judgment, an everlasting reward in the kingdom of Christ, a joyful meeting with the Lord's people in the day of gathering together—these, these are the future prospects of every true Christian. They are all written in the Book—in the Book which is all true.

How striking is the light which the Bible throws on the character of man! It teaches us what men may be expected to be and do in every position and station of life. It gives us the deepest insight into the secret springs and motives of human actions, and the ordinary course of events under the control of human agents. It is the true "discerner of the thoughts and intents of the heart." (Heb. 4:12.) How deep is the wisdom contained in the books of Proverbs and Ecclesiastes! I can well understand an old divine saying, "Give me a candle and a Bible, and shut me up in a dark dungeon, and I will tell you all that the whole world is doing."

Reader, all these are things which men could find nowhere except in the Bible. We have probably not the least idea how little we should know about these things if we had not the Bible. We hardly know the value of the air we breathe, and the Sun which

---

[1] See Exod. 7:10—15:31; 1 Sam. 15:1—31:13; 1 Kings 21:17—22:38; 2 Kings 9:1–37; Acts 1:15–20; 5:1–10.

shines on us, because we have never known what it is to be without them. We do not value the truths on which I have been just now dwelling, because we do not realize the darkness of men to whom these truths have not been revealed. Surely no tongue can fully tell the value of the treasures this one volume contains. Well might old John Newton say that some books were *copper* books in his estimation, some were *silver*, and some few were *gold*—but the Bible alone was like a book all made up of *bank notes*.[1]

Think not for a moment that any part of this precious book is not profitable. Think not that such portions as catalogues and pedigrees, as Leviticus and the description of Ezekiel's temple, are useless and without value. Believe me it is childish folly to question the usefulness of any word in the Bible merely because our eyes at present do not see its use.

Come with me, and look for a moment at the book of nature, and I will soon show you things of which you do not see the use.

Place yourself in imagination by the side of an Australian gold-digging, and observe the earth that is drawn up from its bottom. It is likely that your unpractised eyes will see nothing in that heap but rubbish, and dirt, and stones. And yet that very heap of earth may prove, on washing, to be full of particles of the purest gold. It is just the same with the Bible. We see but a little of it now. We shall find hereafter that every verse of it contained gold.

Place yourself in imagination on the top of some Highland mountain. Look at the minute moss or lichen which clings to the side of that mass of rock. Tell me, if you can, what use and purpose that lichen serves. The birds of the air, the beasts of the field, the very insects, leave it alone. The grouse, the ptarmigan, and red deer draw no sustenance from it. The rock does not require its covering. And yet that minute lichen is as truly a part of God's creation as the cedars of Lebanon, or the *Victoria regia* of the South American rivers. Place it under a microscope, and

---

[1] Before his conversion, John Newton (1725–1807) was an utterly corrupt profligate. Afterwards, however, he entered the Christian ministry and will always be remembered for composing "Amazing Grace," a glorious hymn with the heartfelt line—"that saved a wretch like me." Luke 11:13 & John 7:17 were the texts that led to his conversion.

you will soon see that like all other works of God, it is "very good," and full of beautiful design. (Gen. 1:31.) Settle it down in your mind that as it is with the book of nature, so it is with the book of revelation, the written Word of God. There is not a chapter or verse from first to last which is not in some way profitable. If you and I do not see its use, it is because we have not eyes to see it yet. But all, we may rest assured, is precious. All is "very good." Well said Bishop Jewell, "There is no sentence, no clause, no word, no syllable, no letter, but it is written for thy instruction. There is not one jot but it is signed and sealed with the blood of the Lamb."[1]

Reader, this is the book about which I address you this day. Surely it is no light matter *what you are doing with it*. It is no light matter in what way you are using this treasure. I charge you, I summon you to give an honest answer to my question—What art thou doing with the Bible? Dost thou read it? How READEST THOU?

4. No Book Has Done So Much *for* the World as the Bible

I ask, in the fourth place, because *no book in existence has produced such wonderful effects on mankind at large as the Bible.*

(a) This is the book whose doctrines turned the world upside down in the days of the apostles.

Eighteen centuries have now passed away since God sent forth a few Jews from a remote corner of the Earth to do a work which, according to man's judgment, must have seemed impossible. He sent them forth at a time when the whole world was full of superstition, cruelty, lust, and sin. He sent them forth to proclaim that the established religions of the earth were false and useless, and must be forsaken. He sent them forth to persuade men to give up old habits and customs, and to live different lives. He sent them forth to do battle with vested interests, and old associations, with a bigoted priesthood, with sneering philosophers, with an ignorant population, with bloody-minded emperors, with the whole influence of Rome. Never was there an enterprise to all appearance more Quixotic,[2] and less likely to succeed!

---

[1] John Jewell (1522–1571), Bishop of Salisbury.
[2] Idealistic without regard to practicality.

And how did He arm them for this battle? He gave them no carnal weapons. He gave them no worldly power to compel assent, and no worldly riches to bribe belief. He simply put the Holy Ghost into their hearts, and the Scriptures into their hands. He simply bade them to expound and explain, to enforce and to publish the doctrines of the Bible. The preacher of Christianity in the first century was not a man with a sword and an army, to frighten people, like Mahomet, or a man with a license to be sensual, to allure people, like the priests of the shameful idols of Hindostan. No! he was nothing more than one holy man with one holy book.

And how did these men of one book prosper? In a few generations they entirely changed the face of society by the doctrines of the Bible. They emptied the temples of the heathen gods. They famished idolatry, or left it high and dry like a stranded ship. They brought into the world a higher tone of morality between man and man. They raised the character and position of woman. They altered the standard of purity and decency. They put an end to many cruel and bloody customs, such as the gladiatorial fights. There was no stopping the change. Persecution and opposition were useless. One victory after another was won. One bad thing after another melted away. Whether men liked it or not, they were insensibly affected by the movement of the new religion, and drawn within the whirlpool of its power. The earth shook, and their rotten refuges fell to the ground. The flood rose, and they found themselves obliged to rise with it. The tree of Christianity swelled and grew, and the chains they had cast round it to arrest its growth snapped like tow. And all this was done by the doctrines of the Bible! Talk of victories indeed! What are the victories of Alexander, and Cæsar, and Marlborough, and Napoleon, and Wellington compared with those I have just mentioned? For extent, for completeness, for results, for permanence, there are no victories like the victories of the Bible.

(b) This is the book which turned Europe upside down in the days of the glorious Protestant Reformation.

No man can read the history of Christendom as it was five hundred years ago and not see that darkness covered the whole professing church of Christ, even a darkness that might be felt. So great was the change that had come over Christianity that if an apostle had risen from the dead, he would not have recognised it, and would have thought that heathenism had revived again. The doctrines of the Bible lay buried under a dense mass of human traditions. Penances, and pilgrimages, and indulgences, relic-worship, and image-worship, and saint-worship, and worship of the Virgin Mary, formed the sum and substance of most people's religion. The Church was made an idol. The priests and ministers of the Church usurped the place of Christ. And by what means was all this miserable darkness cleared away? By none so much as by bringing forth once more the Bible.

It was not merely the preaching of Luther and his friends which established Protestantism in Germany. The grand lever which overthrew the Pope's power in that country was Luther's translation of the Bible into the German tongue.[1] It was not merely the writings of Cranmer[2] and the English Reformers which cast down Popery in England. The seeds of the work thus carried forward were first sown by Wycliffe's[3] translation of the Bible many years before. It was not merely the quarrel of Henry VIII and the Pope of Rome which loosened the Pope's hold on English minds. It was the royal permission to have the Bible translated and set up in churches, so that everyone who liked might read it. Yes! it was the reading and circulation of Scripture which mainly established the cause of Protestantism in England, in Germany, and Switzerland. Without it the people would probably have returned to their former bondage when the first Reformers died. But by reading of the Bible the public mind became gradually leavened with the principles of true religion. Men's eyes became thoroughly open. Their spiritual understandings became thoroughly enlarged. The abominations of Popery became distinctly visible. The excellence of the pure gospel became a rooted idea in their hearts. It was then in vain for popes to thunder forth excommunications. It was useless for kings and queens to attempt to stop the course of Protestantism by fire and sword. It

---

[1] Martin Luther (1483–1546), the "father of the Reformation," was the first man to translate the Scriptures into the German language.

[2] Thomas Cranmer (1489–1556), the first Protestant Archbishop of Canterbury, was burnt at the stake during the reign of Mary Tudor.

[3] John Wycliffe (c. 1330–1384), the "Morning Star of the Reformation," was the first man to translate the entire Bible into English.

was all too late. The people knew too much. They had seen the light. They had heard the joyful sound. They had tasted the truth. The Sun had risen on their minds. The scales had fallen from their eyes. The Bible had done its appointed work within them, and that work was not to be overthrown. The people would not return to Egypt. The clock could not be put back again. A mental and moral revolution had been effected, and mainly effected by God's Word. Oh! reader, those are the true revolutions which the Bible effects. What are all the revolutions recorded by Vertot[1]—what are all the revolutions which France and England have gone through, compared to these? No revolutions are so bloodless, none so satisfactory, none so rich in lasting results, as the revolutions accomplished by the Bible!

This is the book on which the well-being of nations has always hinged, and with which the best interests of every nation in Christendom at this moment are inseparably bound up. It is a great fact that the Bible has had a most extraordinary effect on the condition of those nations in which it has been known, taught, and read. Just in proportion as the Bible is honoured or not, light or darkness, morality or immorality, true religion or superstition, liberty or despotism, good laws or bad, will be found in a land. Come with me and open the pages of history, and you will read the proofs in time past. Read it in the history of Israel under the Kings. How great was the wickedness that then prevailed! But who can wonder? The law of the Lord had been completely lost sight of, and was found in the days of Josiah thrown aside in a corner of the temple. (2 Kings 22:8.) Read it in the history of the Jews in our Lord Jesus Christ's time. How awful the picture of scribes and Pharisees, and their religion! But who can wonder? The Scripture was "made of none effect by man's traditions." (Matt. 15:6.) Read it in the history of the Church of Christ in the Middle Ages. What can be worse than the accounts we have of their ignorance and superstition? But who can wonder? The times might well be dark when men had not the light of the Bible.

Come with me next and look at the map of the world, and see what a tale it tells! Which are the countries where the greatest

---

[1] René Aubert de Vertot (1655–1735) was a French historian known for documenting political revolutions.

amount of ignorance, superstition, immorality, and tyranny are to be found at this very moment? The countries in which the Bible is a forbidden or neglected book—such countries as Italy, and Spain, and the South American states. Which are the countries where liberty, and public and private morality, have attained the highest pitch? The countries where the Bible is free to all, like England, Scotland, and the United States. Yes! when you know how a nation deals with the Bible, you may generally know what a nation is. Oh! that the rulers of some nations did but know that a free Bible is the grand secret of national prosperity, and that the surest way to make subjects orderly and obedient is to allow a free passage to the living waters of God's Word! Oh! that the people of some countries did but see that a free Bible is the beginning of all real freedom, and that the first liberty they should seek after is liberty for the apostles and prophets—liberty to have a Bible in every house, and a Bible in every hand! Well said Bishop Hooper,[1] "God in heaven and the king on earth have no greater friend than the Bible." It is a striking fact that when British sovereigns are crowned, they are publicly presented with the Bible, and told, "This book is the most valuable thing this world affords."

This is the book which at this moment is producing the mightiest moral and spiritual effects throughout the world. This is the secret of the wonderful success which attends the London City Mission and the Irish Church Missions. This is the true account of that amazing move towards Protestantism which has lately taken place in several departments of France. Which are the cities of the earth where the fewest soldiers and police are required to keep order? London, Manchester, Liverpool, New York—cities which are deluged with Bibles. Which are the churches on earth which are producing the greatest effect on mankind? The churches in which the Bible is exalted. Which are the parishes in England and Scotland where religion and morality have the strongest hold? The parishes in which the Bible is most circulated and read. Who are the ministers in England who have the most real influence over the minds of the people? Not those who are ever crying "Church! Church!" but those who are faithfully preaching

---

[1] John Hooper (1495–1555), Bishop of Gloucester and martyr.

the Word. Ah! reader, a church which does not honour the Bible is as useless as a body without life, or a steam engine without fire. A minister who does not honour the Bible is as useless as a soldier without arms, a builder without tools, a pilot without compass, or a messenger without tidings. It is cheap and easy work for Roman Catholics, neologians, and friends of secular education to sneer at those who love the Bible. But the Romanist, the neologian, and the friends of mere secular education have never yet shewn us one New Zealand, one Tinnevelly, one Sierra Leone as the fruit of their principles.[1] We only can do that who honour the Bible, and we say these are the works of the Word, and the proofs of its power.

This is the book to which the civilized world is indebted for many of its best and most praiseworthy institutions. Few probably are aware how many are the good things that men have adopted for the public benefit, of which the origin may be clearly traced up to the Bible. It has left lasting marks wherever it has been received. From the Bible are drawn many of the best laws by which society is kept in order. From the Bible has been obtained the standard of morality about truth, honesty, and the relations of man and wife, which prevails among Christian nations, and which, however feebly respected in many cases, makes so great a difference between Christians and heathen. To the Bible we are indebted for that most merciful provision for the poor man, the Sabbath day. To the influence of the Bible we owe nearly every humane and charitable institution in existence. The sick, the poor, the aged, the orphan, the lunatic, the idiot, the blind, were seldom or never thought of before the Bible leavened the world. You may search in vain for any record of institutions for their aid in the histories of Athens or Rome. Ah! reader, many sneer at the Bible, and say the world would get on well enough without it, who little think how great are their own obligations to the Bible. Little does the infidel think, as he lies sick in one of our great hospitals, that he owes all his present comforts to the very book he affects to despise. Had it not been for the Bible, he might have died in misery, uncared for, unno-

---

[1] Three remote missionary colonies founded by evangelicals: New Zealand in the South Pacific, Tinnevelly in southeastern India, and Sierra Leone in western Africa.

ticed, and alone. Verily the world we live in is fearfully unconscious of its debts. The last day alone, I believe, will tell the full amount of benefit conferred upon it by the Bible.

Reader, this wonderful book is the subject about which I address you this day. Surely it is no light matter *what you are doing with the Bible*. The swords of conquering generals, the ship in which Nelson led the fleets of England to victory, the hydraulic press which raised the tubular bridge at the Menai—each and all of these are objects of interest as instruments of mighty power.[1] The book I speak of this day is an instrument a thousandfold mightier still. Surely it is no light matter whether you are paying it the attention it deserves. I charge you, I summon you to give me an honest answer this day—What art thou doing with the Bible? Dost thou read it? How READEST THOU?

5. No Book Can Do So Much as the Bible

I ask, in the fifth place, because *no book in existence can do so much for everyone who reads it rightly as the Bible.*

The Bible does not profess to teach the wisdom of this world. It was not written to explain geology or astronomy. It will neither instruct you in mathematics nor in natural philosophy. It will not make you a doctor, or a lawyer, or an engineer.

But there is another world to be thought of beside that world in which man now lives. There are other ends for which man was created besides making money and working. There are other interests which he is meant to attend to besides those of his body —and those interests are the interests of his soul.

The interests of the immortal soul are the interests which the Bible is especially able to promote. If you would know law, you may study Blackstone or Sugden. If you would know astronomy or geology, you may study Herschel and Lyell.[2] But if you would

---

[1] The HMS *Victory*, an exceptional 100-gun ship of the line, was the flagship of Admiral Horatio Nelson (1758-1805) in the Battle of Trafalgar where twenty French & Spanish ships were destroyed, while not one single British vessel was lost; and the Britannia Bridge (built 1846-49) is a tubular railroad bridge, spanning Menai Strait (Wales), made of two completely enclosed wrought-iron tubes, which were joined in the middle. Capstan and hydraulic power lifted the rectangular tubes into place, each weighing about 1500 tons.

[2] Sir William Blackstone (1723-1780); Edward B. Sugden (1781-1875); Sir William Herschel (1738-1822), Sir Charles Lyell (1797-1875).

know how to have your soul saved, you must study the written Word of God.

Reader, the Bible is *"able to make a man wise unto salvation, through faith which is in Christ Jesus."* (2 Tim. 3:15.) It can show you the way which leads to heaven. It can teach you everything you need to know, point out everything you need to believe, and explain everything you need to do. It can show you what you are —*a sinner.* It can show you what God is—perfectly *holy.* It can show you the great giver of pardon, peace, and grace—*Jesus Christ.* I have read of an Englishman who visited Scotland in the days of Blair, Rutherford, and Dickson[1]—three famous preachers —and heard all three in succession. He said that the first showed him the majesty of God, the second showed him the beauty of Christ, and the third showed him all his heart. It is the glory and beauty of the Bible that it is always teaching these three things, more or less, from the first chapter of it to the last.

The Bible applied to the heart by the Holy Ghost is *the grand instrument by which souls are first converted to God.* That mighty change is generally begun by some text or doctrine of the Word brought home to a man's conscience. In this way the Bible has worked moral miracles by thousands. It has made drunkards become sober, unchaste people become pure, thieves become honest, and violent-tempered people become meek. It has wholly altered the course of men's lives. It has caused their old things to pass away, and made all their ways new. It has taught worldly people to seek first the kingdom of God. It has taught lovers of pleasure to become lovers of God. It has taught the stream of men's affections to run upwards instead of running downwards. It has made them think of heaven, instead of always thinking of earth, and live by faith, instead of living by sight. All this it has done in every part of the world. All this it is doing still. What are the pretended Romish miracles, which weak men believe, compared to all this, even if they were true? Those are the truly great miracles which are yearly worked by the Word.

The Bible applied to the heart by the Holy Ghost is *the chief means by which men are built up and established in the faith,* after their conversion. It is able to cleanse them, to sanctify them, to

---

[1] Robert Blair (1593–1666), Samuel Rutherford (*c.* 1600–1661), David Dickson (*c.* 1583–1663).

instruct them in righteousness, and to furnish them thoroughly for all good works. (Ps. 119:9; John 17:17; 2 Tim. 3:16, 17.) The Spirit ordinarily does these things by the written Word, sometimes by the Word read, and sometimes by the Word preached; but seldom, if ever, without the Word. The Bible can show a believer how to walk in this world so as to please God. It can teach him how to glorify Christ in all the relations of life, and can make him a good master, servant, subject, husband, father, or son. It can enable him to bear afflictions and privations without murmuring, and say, "It is well." (2 Kings 4:23, 26.) It can enable him to look down into the grave, and say, "I fear no evil." (Ps. 23:4.) It can enable him to think on judgment and eternity, and not feel afraid. It can enable him to bear persecution without flinching, and to give up liberty and life rather than deny Christ's truth. Is he drowsy in soul? It can awaken him. Is he mourning? It can comfort him. Is he erring? It can restore him. Is he weak? It can make him strong. Is he in company? It can keep him from evil. Is he alone? It can talk with him. (Prov. 6:22.) All this the Bible can do for all believers—for the least as well as the greatest, for the richest as well as the poorest. It has done it for thousands already, and is doing it for thousands every day.

Reader, the man who has the Bible has everything which is absolutely needful to make him spiritually wise. He needs no priest to break the bread of life for him. He needs no ancient traditions, no writings of the Fathers, no voice of the Church, to guide him into all truth. He has the well of truth open before him, and what can he want more? Yes! though he be shut up alone in a prison, or cast on a desert island—though he never see a church, or minister, or sacrament again—if he has but the Bible, he has got the infallible guide, and wants no other. If he has but the will to read that Bible rightly, it shall certainly teach him the road that leads to heaven. It is here alone that infallibility resides. It is not in the Church. It is not in the councils. It is not in ministers. It is only in the written Word.

(*a*) I know well that many say they have found no saving power in the Bible. They tell us they have tried to read it and have learned nothing from it. They can see in it nothing but hard and deep things. They ask us what we mean by talking of its power.

I answer that the Bible no doubt contains hard things, or else it would not be the Book of God. It contains things hard to comprehend, but only hard because we have not grasp of mind to comprehend them. It contains things above our reasoning powers, but nothing that might not be explained if the eyes of our understanding were not feeble and dim. But is not an acknowledgment of our own ignorance the very cornerstone and foundation of all knowledge? Must not many things be taken for granted in the beginning of every science before we can proceed one step towards acquaintance with it? Do we not require our children to learn many things of which they cannot see the meaning at first? And ought we not then to expect to find "deep things" when we begin studying the Word of God, and yet to believe that if we persevere in reading it, the meaning of many of them will one day be made clear? (1 Cor. 2:10.) No doubt we ought so to expect, and so to believe. We must read with humility. We must take much on trust. We must believe that what we know not now, we shall know hereafter, some part in this world, and all in the world to come.

But I ask that man who has given up reading the Bible, because it contains hard things, whether he did not find many things in it easy and plain. I put it to his conscience, whether he did not see great landmarks and leading principles in it all the way through. I ask him whether the things needful to salvation did not stand out boldly before his eyes, like the lighthouses on English headlands from the Land's End to the mouth of the Thames. What should we think of the captain of a steamer who brought up at night in the entrance of the Channel on the plea that he did not know every parish, and village, and creek, along the British coast? Should we not think him a lazy coward, when the lights on the Lizard, and Eddystone, and the Start, and Portland, and St. Catherine's, and Beachy Head, and Dungeness, and the Forelands were shining forth like so many lamps to guide him up to the river? Should we not say, "Why did you not steer by the great leading lights?" And what ought we to say to the man who gives up reading the Bible, because it contains hard things, when his own state, and the path to heaven, and the way to serve God are all written down clearly and unmistakably, as with a sunbeam? Surely we ought to tell that man that his objections are no better than lazy excuses, and do not deserve to be heard.

(b) I know well that many raise the objection that thousands read the Bible, and are not a whit the better for their reading. And they ask us, when this is the case, what becomes of the Bible's boasted power.

I answer that the reason why so many read the Bible without benefit is plain and simple—they do not read it in the right way. There is generally a right way and a wrong way of doing everything in the world; and just as it is with other things, so it is in the matter of reading the Bible. The Bible is not so entirely different from all other books as to make it of no importance in what spirit and manner you read it. It does not do good, as a matter of course, by merely running our eyes over the print, any more than the sacraments do good by mere virtue of our receiving them. It does not ordinarily do good, unless it is read with humility and earnest prayer. The best steam-engine that was ever built is useless if a man does not know how to work it. The best sundial that was ever constructed will not tell its owner the time of day, if he is so ignorant as to put it up in the shade. Just as it is with that steam engine, and that sundial, so it is with the Bible. When men read it without profit, *the fault is not in the Book, but in themselves.*

I tell the man who doubts the power of the Bible, because many read and are no better for the reading, that the abuse of a thing is no argument against the use of it. I tell him boldly that never did man or woman read that book in a childlike persevering spirit—like the Ethiopian eunuch, and the Bereans—and miss the way to heaven. (Acts 8:28; 17:11.) Yes! many a broken cistern will be exposed to shame in the day of judgment, but there will not rise up one soul who will be able to say that he went thirsting to the Bible and found in it no living water; he searched for truth in the Scriptures, and searching, did not find it. The words which are spoken of Wisdom in the Proverbs are strictly true of the Bible:

> If thou criest after knowledge, and liftest up thy voice for understanding; If thou seekest her as silver, and searchest for her as for hid treasures; Then shalt thou understand the fear of the LORD, and find the knowledge of God. (Prov. 2:3–5)

Reader, this wonderful book is the subject about which I address you this day. Surely it is no light matter *what you are doing with the Bible.* What should you think of the man who, in time of cholera, despised a sure receipt for preserving the health of his body? What must be thought of you, if you despise the only sure receipt for the everlasting health of your soul? I charge you, I entreat you, to give an honest answer to my question. What dost thou do with the Bible? Dost thou read it? HOW READEST THOU?

6. No Book Has Been so Neglected & Misused as the Bible

I ask, in the sixth place, because *no gift of God to man is so awfully neglected and misused as the Bible.*

Man has an unhappy skill in abusing God's gifts. His privileges, and power, and faculties are all ingeniously perverted to other ends than those for which they were bestowed. His speech, his imagination, his intellect, his strength, his time, his influence, his money—instead of being used as instruments for glorifying his Maker—are generally employed for his own selfish ends. And just as man naturally makes a bad use of his other mercies, so he does of the written Word. One sweeping charge may be brought against the whole of Christendom, and that charge is neglect and abuse of the Bible.

Reader, I know that this charge sounds awful. Listen to me, and I will give you proofs to substantiate it. Awful as it is, it is sadly true.

It is true of the Roman Catholic Church, from one end of the world to the other. For six hundred years that unhappy church has waged open war with the Bible, and has laboured incessantly to prevent people reading it. By a rule deliberately passed in the great Council of Trent,[1] by the bulls of Popes, by the encyclical letters of Romish bishops, by the repeated open hostility of Romish priests—the views of the Church of Rome on this subject have been made fully manifest. Of all the numerous and soul-ruining errors of which the Church of Rome is guilty, none is more mischievous and productive of evil than its treatment of the Bible.

---

[1] The Council of Trent (1545–63) is the single most important event in the history of the Roman Catholic Church; to this day Rome has not repudiated any of its decrees.

It is truly fearful to consider how thoroughly at variance God and the Church of Rome are about the Bible. The Lord God has declared positively that Holy Scripture is "profitable," that it is "given for our learning," that it is "able to make men wise unto salvation," that it is "the sword" which a soldier of Christ should be armed with, that it is "a light to our feet," and that all errors arise from ignorance of it.[1] The Church of Rome, on the other hand, has declared positively, in the Council of Trent, that "If the Holy Scriptures be everywhere allowed indiscriminately in the vulgar tongue, more harm than good will arise from it," and that "If any one shall presume to read, or possess, a Bible, without license, he shall not receive absolution, except he first deliver it up." A license to read the Bible! What a blasphemous insult is this! It would sound as well to talk of a license to breathe God's air, or look at God's sun. Well may the Church of Rome be in gross darkness, when it pours such contempt on the written Word.

It is useless to assert, as some do, that statements such as these are not correct. It is useless to tell us that Bibles are openly paraded for sale in Roman Catholic shop windows in English towns. The Church of Rome dares not yet show itself in its true colours in England. It winks at practices contrary to its avowed principles because it suits its purpose to do so. It throws dust in the eyes of simple people, by the appearance of toleration; and so blinds them to its real character. But the Church of Rome at heart is always the same.

Ask any one who has lived in countries on the Continent, where the power of the Pope is unrestrained, and see what he will tell you. Ask any one, especially, who has lived in Italy, and been at Rome, and seen Roman Catholic religion in full bloom, and mark what kind of account he will give you. If a man would know what real pure Presbyterianism is, he must go to Scotland. If he would know what real pure Church-of-Englandism is, he must visit England. If he would know what real, pure, genuine Romanism is, he should go to Italy and Rome.

Is it not a fact that to have or read an Italian Bible is one of the highest crimes an Italian can commit? He may commit adul-

---

[1] See 2 Tim. 3:16; Rom. 15:4; 2 Tim. 3:15; Eph. 6:17; Ps. 119:105.

tery and fornication—he may stab, or lie, or rob, or swear, or cheat—and get absolution from his priest without much difficulty. But woe be to the Italian who dares to have or read God's holy Word! That fact speaks volumes. Let that fact be thoroughly known all over the world.

Is it not a fact that the Bible itself cannot be bought at Rome, unless with immense difficulty, and at an immense price? You may buy books of many other kinds and descriptions—worthless French novels, frivolous Italian poetry, miserable lying accounts of pretended miracles done by pretended saints, prayers to the Virgin Mary, and all manner of literary rubbish. You may buy poisons, daggers, or intoxicating drinks. You may buy relics, and rosaries, and scapulars, and crucifixes. You may buy masses and services to redeem your father's soul from purgatory. But one thing it is almost impossible to buy, and that is the one book needful—the written Word of God. You may easily buy all means and appliances for doing the works of darkness. You cannot buy the grand help for doing the works of light, except at an enormous cost. That fact alone speaks volumes. Oh! that the world would awake and know it! THE BIBLE IS PRACTICALLY A FORBIDDEN BOOK AT ROME.

Ah! reader, it is an awful thought that all these insults to the Bible are perpetrated in the name of Christianity! It is an awful thought that a day of reckoning is yet to come, and that God, the Judge of all, is just as jealous about His *Word*, as about His *name* and *day!* It is an awful thought that even the Emperor of China will rise up in judgment with the Pope, and condemn him; for he has lately decreed that the New Testament is a profitable book, and may be read. It is an awful thought that this Bible-proscribing Church of Rome contains more members than any other church in the world! Surely I have a right to say, no gift from God is so neglected and misused as the Bible.

But the Church of Rome, unhappily, is not the only professedly Christian church whose members are guilty in this matter. The charge of neglecting the Bible is one which may be brought home to the members of Protestant churches also, and among others to the Protestants of England and Scotland in the present day.

I write this statement down with sorrow. I dare say it will be received by some with surprise, if not with incredulity. But I write it down calmly and deliberately, and I am certain it is true.

I am well aware that there are more Bibles in Great Britain at this moment than there ever were since the world began. There is more Bible buying and Bible selling, more Bible printing and Bible distributing, than ever was since England was a nation. We see Bibles in every bookseller's shop—Bibles of every size, price, and style—Bibles great, and Bibles small—Bibles for the rich, and Bibles for the poor. But all this time I fear we are in danger of forgetting that to *have* the Bible is one thing, and to *read* it quite another.

I am firmly persuaded that the Bible of many a man and woman in Great Britain is *never read at all*. In one house it lies in a corner, stiff, cold, glossy, and fresh as it was when it came from the bookseller's shop. In another it lies on a table, with its owner's name written in it—a silent witness against him day after day. In another it lies on some high shelf, neglected and dusty, to be brought down only on grand occasions, such as a birth in the family, like a heathen idol at its yearly festival. In another it lies deep down at the bottom of some box or drawer, among the things not wanted, and is never dragged forth into the light of day, until the arrival of sickness, the doctor, and death. Ah! these things are sad and solemn. But they are true.

I am firmly persuaded that many in Great Britain who read the Bible *do not read it aright*. One man looks over a chapter on Sunday evening—but that is all. Another reads a chapter every day to his servants at family prayers—but that is all. A third goes a step further and hastily reads a verse or two in private every morning, before he goes out of his house. A fourth goes further still and reads as much as a chapter or two every day, though he does it in a great hurry, and omits it on the smallest pretext. But each and every one of these men does what he does in a heartless, scrambling, formal kind of way. He does it coldly as a duty. He does not do it with appetite and pleasure. He is glad when the task is over. He forgets it all when the book is shut. Oh! what a sad picture is this! But in multitudes of cases, oh! how true.

But how do I know all this? What makes me speak so confidently? Listen to me a few moments and I will lay before you some evidence. Neglect of the Bible is like disease of the body. It shows itself in the face of a man's conduct. It tells it own tale. It cannot be hid.

I am sure that many neglect the Bible, *because of the enormous ignorance of true religion which everywhere prevails.* There are thousands of professing Christians in this Protestant country who know literally nothing about the gospel. They could not give you the slightest account of its distinctive doctrines. They have no more idea of the meaning of conversion, grace, faith, justification, and sanctification than of so many words and names in Arabic. If you were to ask them whether regeneration, and the new creature, were a beast, a man, or a doctrine, they could not tell. And can I suppose such persons read the Scriptures? I cannot suppose it. I do not believe they do.

I am sure that many neglect the Bible, *because of the utter indifference with which they regard false doctrine.* They will talk with perfect coolness of others having become Roman Catholics, or Socinians, or Mormonites, as if it were all the same thing in the long run. And can I suppose such persons search the Scriptures? I cannot suppose it. I do not believe they do.

I am sure that many neglect the Bible, *because of the readiness with which they receive false doctrines.* They are led astray by the first preacher of lies they meet with, who has a pleasant voice, a nice manner, and a gift of eloquent speech. They swallow all he says without enquiry, and believe him as implicitly as Papists do the Pope. And can I suppose such persons search the Scriptures? I cannot suppose it. I do not believe they do.

I am sure that many neglect the Bible, *because of the bitterness with which they contend for some little secondary unimportant point in religion.* They make a "Shibboleth" of their own little cherished point, and are ready to set down every one as "no Christian," if he does not see it with their eyes. (Judg. 12:6.) And can I suppose such persons really search the whole Scriptures? I cannot suppose it. I do not believe they do.

I am sure that many neglect the Bible, *because of the very scanty knowledge they have of its contents.* They know a certain set of doctrines. They can repeat a certain string of hackneyed texts. But they never seem to get beyond this little string. Let a man talk to them about some text out of their beaten path, and he is at once out of their depth. They listen, but have nothing to say.

Let a minister preach to them anything but the merest elements of Christianity, and they appear shocked at him as a rash and unsound teacher. In short, they seem content to remain in the condition described by St. Paul to the Hebrews: always unskilful in the word of righteousness—always in a state of religious babyhood. And can I suppose such persons really search the Scriptures? I cannot suppose it. I do not believe they do.

I am sure that many neglect the Bible, *because of the lives they live.* They do the very things that God plainly forbids. They neglect the very things that God plainly commands. They break God's laws week after week without shame. And can I suppose such persons search the Scriptures? I allow that much knowledge of the Bible and much wickedness of heart may sometimes be found together. But when I see a wicked life, I generally believe there is a neglected Bible.

I am sure that many neglect the Bible, *because of the deaths they die.* They send for a minister in their last moments, and ask for the "consolations of religion." And in what state are they found? They know nothing whatever of the way of salvation. They have to be told which are the first principles of the gospel of Christ. And can I suppose such persons have searched the Scriptures? I cannot suppose it. I do not believe they have.

I bring forward all this evidence with sorrow. I know well it will be offensive to some. But I believe I have stated nothing but glaring facts, which every true Christian and true minister of Christ's gospel will readily confirm. And I say that these facts prove the existence of a sore evil in Great Britain—I mean a neglected Bible. These things would never be, if the Bible was thoroughly *read* by many, as well as *possessed.*

Ah! reader, it is a painful thought that there should be so much profession of love to the Bible among us, and so little proof that the Bible is read! Here we are, as a nation, pluming ourselves on our Protestantism, and yet neglecting the foundation on which Protestantism is built! Here we are, thanking God with our lips, like the Pharisee, that we are not Papists, as some are, and yet dishonouring God's Word! It is an awful thought that the people of this country will be judged according to their light, and that so many of them should be keeping that light under a bushel! Truly I have cause for saying, no gift of God is so neglected as the Bible.

38   J.C. RYLE

Reader, this neglected book is the subject about which I address you this day. Surely it is no light matter *what you are doing with the Bible*. Surely when the plague is abroad, you should search and see whether the plague-spot is on you.[1] I charge you, I entreat you, to give an honest answer to my question. What art thou doing with the Bible? Dost thou read it? How READEST THOU?

7. The Bible is the Only Rule

I ask, in the seventh place, because *the Bible is the only rule by which all questions of doctrine or of duty can be tried.*

The Lord God knows the weakness and infirmity of our poor fallen understandings. He knows that, even after conversion, our perceptions of right and wrong are exceedingly indistinct. He knows how artfully Satan can gild error with an appearance of truth, and can dress up wrong with plausible arguments, till it looks like right. Knowing all this, He has mercifully provided us with an unerring standard of truth and error, right and wrong, and has taken care to make that standard a written book—even the Scripture.

No one can look round the world, and not see the wisdom of such a provision. No one can live long, and not find out that he is constantly in need of a counsellor and adviser—of a rule of faith and practice, on which he can depend. Unless he lives like a beast, without a soul and conscience, he will find himself constantly assailed by difficult and puzzling questions. He will be often asking himself, What must I believe? and what must I do?

(a) The world is full of difficulties about points of *doctrine*. The house of error lies close alongside the house of truth. The door of one is so like the door of the other that there is continual risk of mistakes.

Does a man read or travel much? He will soon find the most opposite opinions prevailing among those who are called Christians. He will discover that different persons give the most different answers to the important question, "What shall I do to be

---

[1] In fatal cases of bubonic plague, within six days of being biten the victim develops a blackish pustule at the point of infection. Death results in about four days. The deep purple, which appears in all plague victims during their last hours, is due to respiratory failure; hence the name "Black Death."

saved?" (Acts 16:30.) The Roman Catholic and the Protestant, the neologian and the Tractarian, the Mormonite and the Swedenborgian—each and all will assert that he alone has the truth. Each and all will tell him that safety is only to be found in his party. Each and all say, "Come with us." (Prov. 1:11.) All this is puzzling. What shall a man do?

Does he settle down quietly in some English or Scotch parish? He will soon find that even in our own land the most conflicting views are held. He will soon discover that there are serious differences among Christians, as to the comparative importance of the various parts and articles of the faith. One man thinks of nothing but church government; another of nothing but sacraments, services, and forms; a third of nothing but preaching the gospel. Does he apply to ministers for a solution? He will perhaps find one minister teaching one doctrine, and another another. Does he go to the bishops for help? He will find what one bishop says is right, another says is wrong. All this is puzzling. What shall a man do?

There is only one answer to this question. A man must make the Bible alone his rule. He must <u>receive nothing</u>, and <u>believe nothing</u>, <u>which is not according to the Word.</u> He must try all religious teaching by one simple test—Does it square with the Bible? What saith the Scripture?

I would to God the eyes of the laity of this country were more open on this subject. I would to God they would learn to weigh sermons, books, opinions, and ministers, in the scales of the Bible, and to value all according to their conformity to the Word. I would to God they would see that it matters little who says a thing—whether he be Father or Reformer, bishop or archbishop, priest or deacon, archdeacon or dean. The only question is—Is the thing said scriptural? If it is, it ought to be received and believed. If it is not, it ought to be refused and cast aside. I fear the consequences of that servile acceptance of everything which the "parson says," which is so common among many English laymen. I fear lest they be led they know not whither, like the blinded Syrians, and awake some day to find themselves in the power of Rome. (2 Kings 6:20.) Oh! that men in England would only remember for what purpose the Bible was given them!

I tell English laymen that it is nonsense to say, as some do, that it is presumptuous to judge a minister's teaching by the Word. When one doctrine is proclaimed in one parish, and another in another, people must read and judge for themselves. Both doctrines cannot be right, and both ought to be tried by the Word. I charge them, above all things, never to suppose that any true minister of the gospel will dislike his people measuring all he teaches by the Bible. On the contrary, the more they read the Bible, and prove all he says by the Bible, the better he will be pleased. A false minister may say, "You have no right to use your private judgment: leave the Bible to us who are ordained." A true minister will say, "Search the Scriptures, and if I do not teach you what is scriptural, do not believe me." A false minister may cry, "Hear the Church," and "Hear me." A true minister will say, "Hear the Word of God." (Luke 11:28.)

(b) But the world is not only full of difficulties about points of doctrine. It is equally full of difficulties about points of *practice*. Every professing Christian, who wishes to act conscientiously, must know that it is so. The most puzzling questions are continually arising. He is tried on every side by doubts as to the line of duty, and can often hardly see what is the right thing to do.

He is tried by questions connected with the management of his *worldly calling*, if he is in business or in trade. He sometimes sees things going on of a very doubtful character—things that can hardly be called fair, straightforward, truthful, and doing as you would be done by. But then everybody in the trade does these things. They have always been done in the most respectable houses. There would be no carrying on a profitable business if they were not done. They are not things distinctly named and prohibited by God. All this is very puzzling. What is a man to do?

He is tried by questions of a *political kind*, if he occupies a high position in life. He finds that men do things in their public capacity which they would not think of doing in their private one. He finds that men are expected to sacrifice their own judgment, private opinion, and conscience, to the interests of their own party, and to believe that the acts of their own political friends are always right, and the acts of their political opponents always wrong. All this is puzzling. What is a man to do?

He is tried by questions in the matter of *speaking truth*. He hears things said continually which he knows are not correct. He hears a false colouring put on stories, which he knows ought to wear a different aspect. He sees additions to, and subtractions from, the whole truth. He sees evasions, and equivocations, and concealments of facts in every class of society, when self-interests are at stake. He hears false compliments paid, and false excuses alleged, and false characters given. But then it is the way of the world. Everybody does so. Nobody means any harm by it. All this is very puzzling. What is he to do?

He is tried by questions about *sabbath observance*. Can there really be any harm in travelling, or writing letters, or keeping accounts, or reading newspapers on Sunday? Is it wrong to take a situation on a railway, merely because the Sunday traffic would almost entirely keep him away from public worship? Would it be wrong to open the Crystal Palace at Sydenham on Sundays? Is not Christianity a religion of liberty? Do not many learned, and respectable, and titled people think that Sunday should be a day for recreation? All this is very puzzling. What is a man to do?

He is tried by questions about *worldly amusements*. Races, and balls, and operas, and theatres, and card parties are all very doubtful methods of spending time. But he sees numbers of great people taking part in them. Are all these people wrong? Can there really be such mighty harm in these things? All this is very puzzling. What is a man to do?

He is tried by questions about the *education of his children*. He wishes to train them up morally and religiously, and to remember their souls. But he is told by many sensible people that young persons will be young, that it does not do to check and restrain them too much, and that he ought to attend pantomimes and children's parties, and give children's balls himself. He is informed that this nobleman, or that lady of rank, always does so, and yet they are reckoned religious people. Surely it cannot be wrong. All this is very puzzling. What is he to do?

He is tried by questions about *reading*. He does not wish to read what is really bad, and has not time for much reading beside the Bible. Ought he, or ought he not, to read such things as sceptical writings, or French novels, or semi-popish poetry? Can there really be much harm in it? Do not many persons, as good as himself, read these things? And after all, the Bible has not expressly forbidden Emerson or Eugéne Sue. All this is very puzzling. What is he to do?

There is only one answer to all these questions. A man must make the Bible his rule of conduct. He must make its leading principles the compass by which he steers his course through life. By the letter or spirit of the Bible he must test every difficult point and question. *"To the law, and to the testimony! What saith the Scripture?"* He ought to care nothing for what other people may think right. He ought not to set his watch by the clock of his neighbour, but by the sundial of the Word. (Isa. 8:20; Rom. 4:3; Gal. 4:30.)

Reader, I charge you solemnly to act on the maxim I have just laid down, and to adhere to it rigidly all the days of your life. You will never repent of it. Make it a leading principle never to act contrary to the Word. Care not for the charge of overstrictness and needless precision. Remember, you serve a strict and holy God. Listen not to the common objection that the rule you have laid down is impossible, and cannot be observed in such a world as this. Let those who make such an objection speak out plainly, and tell us for what purpose the Bible was given to man. Let them remember that by the Bible we shall all be judged at the last day, and let them learn to judge themselves by it here, lest they be judged and condemned by it hereafter.

Reader, this mighty rule of faith and practice is the book about which I am addressing you this day. Surely it is no light matter *what you are doing with the Bible.* Surely when danger is abroad on the right hand and on the left, you should consider what you are doing with the safeguard which God has provided. I charge you, I beseech you, to give an honest answer to my question. What art thou doing with the Bible? Dost thou read it? HOW READEST THOU?

8. All True Servants of God Love the Bible

I ask, in the next place, because *the Bible is the book which all true servants of God have always lived on and loved.*

Every living thing which God creates requires food. The life that God imparts needs sustaining and nourishing. It is so with animal and vegetable life—with birds, beasts, fishes, reptiles, insects, and plants. It is equally so with spiritual life. When the Holy Ghost raises a man from the death of sin, and makes him a new creature in Christ Jesus, the new principle in that man's heart requires food, and the only food which will sustain it is the Word of God.

There never was a man or woman truly converted, from one end of the world to the other, who did not love the revealed will of God. Just as a child born into the world desires naturally the milk provided for its nourishment, so does a soul "born again" desire the sincere milk of the Word. (1 Pet. 1:23; 2:2.) This is a common mark of all the children of God—they "delight in the law of the LORD." (Ps. 1:2.)

Show me a person who despises Bible reading, or thinks little of Bible preaching, and I hold it to be a certain fact that he is not yet "born again." He may be zealous about forms and ceremonies. He may be diligent in attending sacraments and daily services. But if these things are more precious to him than the Bible, I cannot think he is a converted man. Tell me what the Bible is to a man, and I will generally tell you what he is. This is the pulse to try—this is the barometer to look at—if we would know the state of the heart. I have no notion of the Spirit dwelling in a man and not giving clear evidence of His presence. And I believe it to be a signal evidence of the Spirit's presence when the Word is really precious to a man's soul.

Love to the Word is one of the characteristics we see in Job. Little as we know of this patriarch and his age, this at least stands out clearly. He says, "I have esteemed the words of His mouth more than my necessary food." (Job 23:12.)

Love to the Word is a shining feature in the character of David. Mark how it appears all through that wonderful part of Scripture, the One hundred nineteenth Psalm. He might well say, "O how love I Thy law"! (Ps. 119:97.)

Love to the Word is a striking point in the character of St. Paul. What were he and his companions but men "mighty in the Scriptures"? (Acts 18:24.) What were his sermons but expositions and applications of the Word?

Love to the Word appears preëminently in our Lord and Saviour Jesus Christ. He read it publicly. He quoted it continually. He expounded it frequently. He advised the Jews to "search" it.

(John 5:39.) He used it as His weapon to resist the devil. He said repeatedly, "The Scripture must be fulfilled." (Mark 14:49.) Almost the last thing He did was to "open the understanding of His disciples, that they might understand the Scriptures." (Luke 24:45.) Ah! reader, that man can be no true servant of Christ, who has not something of his Master's mind and feeling toward the Bible.

Love to the Word has been a prominent feature in the history of all the saints, of whom we know anything, since the days of the apostles. This is the lamp which Athanasius, and Chrysostom, and Augustine followed. This is the compass which kept the Vallenses from making shipwreck of the faith. This is the well which was reopened by Wycliffe and Luther, after it had been long stopped up. This is the sword with which Latimer, and Jewell, and Knox won their victories. This is the manna which fed Baxter, and Owen, and the noble host of the Puritans, and made them strong to battle. This is the armoury from which Whitefield and Wesley drew their powerful weapons. This is the mine from which Bickersteth and M'Cheyne brought forth rich gold.[1] Differing as these holy men did in some matters, on one point they were all agreed—they all delighted in the Word.

Love to the Word is one of the first things that appears in the converted heathen, at the various missionary stations throughout the world. In hot climates and in cold, among savage people and among civilized, in New Zealand, in the South Sea Islands, in Africa, in Hindostan—it is always the same. They enjoy hearing it read. They long to be able to read it themselves. They wonder

---

[1] These men represent a sweep through Church history: Athanasius (c. 293–373), Chrysostom (c. 354–407), and Augustine (354–430) are known as "church fathers." The Vallenses were French proto-Protestants from the Middle Ages; John Wycliffe (c. 1330–1384) was the first man to translate the Bible into English. Martin Luther (1483–1546) was the German theologian who initiated the Protestant Reformation. Hugh Latimer (1485–1555), John Jewell (1522–1571), and John Knox (c. 1514–1572) were instrumental in shaping the English & Scottish reformations. Richard Baxter (1615–1691) and John Owen (1616–1683) were two leaders of Puritanism, a movement committed to the purity & reformation of the Church. George Whitefield (1714–1770) and John Wesley (1703–1791) were brilliant preachers during the Great Awakening. And Edward Bickersteth (1786–1850) and Robert M'Cheyne (1813–1843) were faithful ministers of the gospel, whose lives bring the survey to the period when J.C. Ryle first published this tract (1852).

why Christians did not send it to them before. How striking is the picture which Moffat draws of Africaner, the fierce South African chieftain, when first brought under the power of the gospel! "Often have I seen him," he says, "under the shadow of a great rock nearly the livelong day, eagerly perusing the pages of the Bible."[1] How touching is the expression of a poor converted Negro, speaking of the Bible! He said, "It is never old and never cold." How affecting was the language of another old Negro, when some would have dissuaded him from learning to read, because of his great age. "No!" he said, "I will never give it up till I die. It is worth all the labour to be able to read that one verse, 'God so loved the world, that He gave His only begotten Son, that whosoever believeth in Him should not perish, but have eternal life.'" (John 3:16.)

Love to the Bible is one of the grand points of agreement among all converted men and women in our land. Episcopalians and Presbyterians, Baptists and Independents, Methodists and Plymouth Brethren—all unite in honouring the Bible, as soon as they are real Christians. This is the manna which all the tribes of our Israel feed upon, and find satisfying food. This is the fountain round which all the various portions of Christ's flock meet together, and from which no sheep goes thirsty away. Oh! that believers in this country would learn to cleave more closely to the written Word? Oh! that they would see that the more the Bible, and the Bible only, is the substance of man's religion, the more they agree! It is probable there never was an uninspired book more universally admired than Bunyan's *Pilgrim's Progress*.[2] It is a book which all denominations of Christians delight to honour. It has won praise from all parties. Now what a striking fact it is that the author was preëminently a man of one book! He had read hardly anything but the Bible.

---

[1] Robert Moffat (1795–1883), Scottish missionary & translator of the Bible, brought the Word of God to Christian Africaner (d. 1822), chief of the Oorlams (Khoi) people. Africaner's conversion was said to be the eighth wonder of the world, because of his savage past.

[2] John Bunyan (1628–1688) was a self-taught preacher of the gospel who spent twelve years in jail as persecution for his faith. During his imprisonment he wrote *The Pilgrim's Progress* (1678, 1684), an allegorical tale of the Christian walk. Ten editions were printed during Bunyan's lifetime, and it eventually became the most widely read book in English, next to the Bible.

Away with the foolish idea that making the Bible alone the rule of faith hinders unity, and that those who profess to glory in the Bible, and nothing but the Bible, are hopelessly divided! It is a weak invention of the enemy. It is a base calumny. No doubt there is much dissension and party spirit among mere outward professors; but among the great bulk of believing Protestants there is a wonderful amount of unity—real, thorough, and deep, far deeper than the boasted unity of Rome. Their differences are merely about the outward trappings of Christianity. About the body of the faith they are all agreed. Their differences are studiously exaggerated by the enemies of true religion. Their points of agreement—such as the *Harmony of Protestant Confessions* exhibits —are studiously kept out of sight. Their differences are differences which in times of common danger are soon forgotten. Their unity is an unity which, in front of sin, heathenism, and persecution, stands boldly out. Ridley and Hooper forgot their old disagreements when they found themselves in Queen Mary's prisons.[1] Churchmen and Nonconformists laid aside their quarrels when James II tried to bring back Popery to England. Protestant missionaries, of different denominations, find they can work and pray together, when they are in the midst of idolaters. Protestant believers in London have proved to the world that they can agree to labour together for the conversion of souls, maintaining that glorious institution, the London City Mission. And what is the secret of all this deep-seated unity? It comes from this —That all believers on earth are not only born of one Spirit, but also read one holy book, and feed on the bread of one Bible.

Ah! reader, it is a blessed thought that there will be "much people" in heaven at last. Few as the Lord's people undoubtedly are at any given time or place, yet all gathered together at last, they will be "a multitude that no man can number." (Rev. 19:1; 7:9.) They will be of one heart and mind. They will have passed through like experience. They will all have repented, believed, lived holy, prayerful, and humble. They will all have washed their robes and made them white in the blood of the Lamb. But one thing beside all this they will have in common. They will all love

---

[1] John Hooper (1495-1555), Bishop of Gloucester, and Nicholas Ridley (*c.* 1500-1555), Bishop of Rochester & London, were martyred during the reign of Mary Tudor, Queen of England.

the texts and doctrines of the Bible. The Bible will have been their food and delight, in the days of their pilgrimage on earth. And the Bible will be a common subject of joyful meditation and retrospect, when they are gathered together in heaven.

Reader, this book, which all true Christians live upon and love, is the subject about which I am addressing you this day. Surely it is no light matter *what you are doing with the Bible*. Surely it is matter for serious inquiry, whether you know anything of this love to the Word, and have this mark of "walking in the footsteps of the flock." (Song of Solomon 1:8.) I charge you, I entreat you, to give me an honest answer. What art thou doing with the Bible? Dost thou read it? How READEST THOU?

9. Only the Bible Can Comfort a Dying Man

I ask, in the last place, because *the Bible is the only book which can comfort a man in the last hours of his life.*

Death is an event which in all probability is before us all. There is no avoiding it. It is the river which each of us must cross. I who write, and you who read, have each one day to die. It is good to remember this. We are all sadly apt to put away the subject from us. "Each man thinks each man mortal but himself."[1] I want every one to do his duty in life, but I also want every one to think of death. I want everyone to know how to live, but I also want everyone to know how to die.

Death is a solemn event to all. It is the winding up of all earthly plans and expectations. It is a separation from all we have loved and lived with. It is often accompanied by much bodily pain and distress. It brings us to the grave, the worm, and corruption. It opens the door to judgment and eternity—to heaven or to hell. It is an event after which there is no change, or space for repentance. Other mistakes may be corrected or retrieved, but not a mistake on our deathbeds. As the tree falls, there it must lie. No conversion in the coffin! No new birth after we have ceased to breathe! And death is before us all. It may be close at hand. The time of our departure is quite uncertain. But sooner or later we must each lie down alone and die. All these are serious considerations.

---

[1] Edward Young (1683–1765), *The Complaint: or Night Thoughts on Life, Death, & Immortality* (1742–1745).

Death is a solemn event, even to the believer in Christ. For him no doubt the "sting of death" is taken away. (1 Cor. 15:55.) Death has become one of his privileges, for he is Christ's. Living or dying, he is the Lord's. If he lives, Christ lives in him; and if he dies, he goes to live with Christ. To him "to live is Christ, and to die is gain." (Phil. 1:21.) Death frees him from many trials—from a weak body, a corrupt heart, a tempting devil, and an ensnaring or persecuting world. Death admits him to the enjoyment of many blessings. He rests from his labours—the hope of a joyful resurrection is changed into a certainty; he has the company of holy redeemed spirits—he is "with Christ." (Phil. 1:23.) All this is true; and yet, even to a believer, death is a solemn thing. Flesh and blood naturally shrink from it. To part from all we love is a wrench and trial to the feelings. The world we go to is a world unknown, even though it is our home. Friendly and harmless as death is to a believer, it is not an event to be treated lightly. It always must be a very solemn thing.

Reader, it becomes every one to consider calmly how he is going to meet death. Gird up your loins, like a man, and look the subject in the face. Listen to me while I tell you a few things about the end to which we are coming.

The good things of the world cannot comfort a man when he draws near death. All the gold of California and Australia will not provide light for the dark valley. Money can buy the best medical advice and attendance for a man's body. But money cannot buy peace for his conscience, heart, and soul.

Relatives, loved friends, and servants cannot comfort a man when he draws near death. They may minister affectionately to his bodily wants. They may watch by his bedside tenderly, and anticipate his every wish. They may smooth down his dying pillow, and support his sinking frame in their arms. But they cannot "minister to a mind diseased."[1] They cannot stop the achings of a troubled heart. They cannot screen an uneasy conscience from the eye of God.

The pleasures of the world cannot comfort a man when he draws near death. The brilliant ballroom, the merry dance, the midnight revel, the party to Epsom races, the card table, the box

---

[1] William Shakespeare (1564–1616), *Macbeth*, V, III, 40 (1606?).

at the opera, the voices of singing men and singing women—all these are at length distasteful things. To hear of hunting and shooting engagements gives him no pleasure. To be invited to feasts, and regattas, and fancy fairs gives him no ease. He cannot hide from himself that these are hollow, empty, powerless things. They jar upon the ear of his conscience. They are out of harmony with his condition. They cannot stop one gap in his heart, when the last enemy is coming in like a flood. They cannot make him calm in the prospect of meeting a holy God.

Books and newspapers cannot comfort a man when he draws near death. The most brilliant writings of Macaulay or Dickens will pall upon his ear. The most able article in the *Times* will fail to interest him. The *Edinburgh* and *Quarterly* reviews will give him no pleasure. *Punch* and the *Illustrated News*, and the last new novel, will lie unopened and unheeded. Their time will be past. Their vocation will be gone. Whatever they may be in health, they are useless in the hour of death.

There is but one fountain of comfort for a man drawing near to his end, and that is the Bible. Chapters out of the Bible, texts out of the Bible, statements of truth taken out of the Bible, books containing matter drawn from the Bible—these are a man's only chance of comfort when he comes to die. I do not at all say that the Bible will do good, as a matter of course, to a dying man, if he has not valued it before. I know, unhappily, too much of deathbeds to say that. I do not say whether it is probable that he who has been unbelieving and neglectful of the Bible in life will at once believe and get comfort from it in death. But I do say positively that no dying man will ever get real comfort, except from the contents of the Word of God. All comfort from any other source is a house built upon sand.

I lay this down as a rule of universal application. I make no exception in favour of any class on earth. Kings and poor men, learned and unlearned—all are on a level in this matter. There is not a jot of real consolation for any dying man, unless he gets it from the Bible. Chapters, passages, texts, promises, and doctrines of Scripture—heard, received, believed, and rested on—these are the only comforters I dare promise to any one, when he leaves the world. Taking the sacrament will do a man no more good than the Popish extreme unction, so long as the Word is not received and believed. Priestly absolution will no more ease the conscience than the incantations of a heathen magician, if the poor dying sinner does not receive and believe Bible truth. I tell everyone who reads this paper that, although men may seem to get on comfortably without the Bible while they live, they may be sure that without the Bible they cannot comfortably die. It was a true confession of the learned Selden, "There is no book upon which we can rest in a dying moment but the Bible."[1]

I might easily confirm all I have just said by examples and illustrations. I might show you the deathbeds of men who have affected to despise the Bible. I might tell you how Voltaire and Paine—the famous infidels—died in misery, bitterness, rage, fear, and despair.[2] I might show you the happy deathbeds of those who have loved the Bible and believed it, and the blessed effect the sight of their deathbeds had on others. Cecil[3]—a minister whose praise ought to be in all churches—says, "I shall never forget standing by the bedside of my dying mother. 'Are you afraid to die?' I asked. 'No!' she replied. 'But why does the uncertainty of another state give you no concern?' 'Because God has said, "Fear not; when thou passest through the waters I will be with thee, and through the rivers, they shall not overflow thee."'" (Isa. 43:2.) I might easily multiply illustrations of this kind. But I think it better to conclude this part of my subject by giving the result of my own observations as a minister.

I have seen not a few dying persons in my time. I have seen great varieties of manner and deportment among them. I have

---

[1] John Selden (1584–1654) was a leading lay-member of the Westminster Assembly. Near the end of his life his soul found rest in Titus 2:11–15.

[2] Voltaire (1694–1778), Frenchman, writer, philosopher, and reprobate, was as wretched in death as he was in life. Upon his deathbed he cried out, "I am abandoned by God and man! I will give you half of what I am worth if you will give me six months' life. Then I shall go to hell; and you will go with me. O Christ! O Jesus Christ!" The nurse who attended him said, "For all the wealth in Europe I would not see another infidel die."

Anglo-American writer Thomas Paine (1737–1809) fared little better than the Frenchman on his deathbed. He said, "O Lord, help me! Christ, help me! O God, what have I done to suffer so much? But there is no God! But if there should be, what will become of me hereafter? Stay with me, for God's sake! Send even a child to stay with me, for it is hell to be alone. If ever the devil had an agent, I have been that one."

[3] Richard Cecil (1748–1810).

seen some die sullen, silent, and comfortless. I have seen others die ignorant, unconcerned, and apparently without much fear. I have seen some die so wearied with long illness that they were quite willing to depart, and yet they did not seem to me at all in a fit state to go before God. I have seen others die with professions of hope and trust in God, without leaving satisfactory evidences that they were on the rock. I have seen others die who, I believe, were "in Christ"[1] and safe, and yet they never seemed to enjoy much sensible comfort. I have seen some few dying in the full assurance of hope, and like Bunyan's "Standfast," giving glorious testimony to Christ's faithfulness, even in the river.[2] But one thing I have never seen. I never saw any one enjoy what I should call real, solid, calm, reasonable peace on his deathbed, who did not draw his peace from the Bible. And this I am bold to say, that the man who thinks to go to his deathbed without having the Bible for his comforter, his companion, and his friend, is one of the greatest madmen in the world. There are no comforts for the soul but Bible comforts, and he who has not got hold of these, has got hold of nothing at all, unless it be a broken reed.

Reader, the only comforter for a deathbed is the book about which I address you this day. Surely it is no light matter whether you read that book or not. Surely a dying man, in a dying world, should seriously consider whether he has got anything to comfort him, when his turn comes to die. I charge you, I entreat you, for the last time, to give an honest answer to my question. What art thou doing with the Bible? Dost thou read it? How READEST THOU?

[1] Rom. 8:1; 2 Cor. 5:17.

[2] "'My toilsome days are ended. I am going now to see that head that was crowned with thorns, and that face that was spit upon for me. I have formerly lived by hearsay and faith, but now I go where I shall live by sight, and shall be with him in whose company I delight myself. I have loved to hear my Lord spoken of, and wherever I have seen the print of his shoe in the earth, there I have coveted to set my foot too. His name has been to me as a civit-box, yea, sweeter than all perfumes. His voice to me has been most sweet, and his countenance I have more desired than they that have most desired the light of the Sun. His word I did use to gather for my food, and for antidotes against my faintings. He has held me, and hath kept me from mine iniquities, yea, my steps hath he strengthened in his way.'" (Mr. Standfast's last words in *The Pilgrim's Progress* [1678, 1684], by John Bunyan.)

10. Conclusion

Reader, I have now given you the reasons why I ask you a question about the Bible on the present occasion. I have shown you that knowledge of the Bible is absolutely necessary to salvation; that no book is written in such a manner as the Bible; that no book contains such matter; that no book has done so much for the world generally; that no book can do so much for everyone who reads it aright; that no book is so awfully neglected; that this book is the only rule of faith and practice; that it is, and always has been, the food of all true servants of God; and that it is the only book which can comfort men when they die. All these are ancient things. I do not pretend to tell you anything new. I have only gathered together old truths, and tried to mould them into a new shape. Let me finish all, by addressing a few plain words to the conscience of every class of readers.

(1) These pages may fall into the hands of some who can read, but never do read the Bible at all. Reader, are you one of them? If you are, I have something to say to you.

I cannot comfort you in your present state of mind. It would be mockery and deceit to do so. I cannot speak to you of peace and heaven, while you treat the Bible as you do. You are in danger of losing your soul.

You are in danger, because *your neglected Bible is a plain evidence that you do not love God.* The health of a man's body may generally be known by his appetite. The health of a man's soul may be known by his treatment of the Bible. Now you are manifestly labouring under a sore disease. Reader, will you not repent?

You are in danger, because *God will reckon with you for your neglect of the Bible in the day of judgment.* You will have to give account of your use of time, strength, and money; and you will also have to give account of your use of the Word. You will not stand at that bar side by side with the Patagonian, who never heard of the Bible. Oh, no! To whom much is given, of them much will be required. Of all men's buried talents, none will weigh them down so heavily as a neglected Bible. As you deal with the Bible, so God will deal with your soul. Reader, I say again, will you not repent, and turn over a new leaf in life, and read your Bible?

You are in danger, because *there is no degree of error in religion into which you may not fall.* You are at the mercy of the first clever Jesuit, Mormonite, Socinian, Turk, or Jew, who may happen to meet you. A land of unwalled villages is not more defenceless against an enemy than the man who neglects his Bible. You may go on tumbling from one step of delusion to another, till at length you are landed in the pit of hell. Reader, I say once more, will you not repent and read your Bible?

You are in danger, because *there is not a single reasonable excuse you can allege for neglecting the Bible.* You have no time to read it forsooth! But you can make time for eating, drinking, sleeping, and perhaps for newspaper reading and smoking. You might easily make time to read the Word. Alas! it is not want of time, but waste of time that ruins souls. You find it too troublesome to read forsooth! You had better say at once it is too much trouble to go to heaven, and you are content to go to hell. Truly these excuses are like the rubbish round the walls of Jerusalem in Nehemiah's days. They would all soon disappear if, like the Jews, you had "a mind to work." (Neh. 4:6.) Reader, I say for the last time, will you not repent and read your Bible?

I know I cannot reach your heart. I cannot make you see and feel these things. I can only enter my solemn protest against your present treatment of the Bible, and lay that protest before your conscience. I do so with all my soul. Oh! beware lest you repent too late! Beware lest you put off seeking for the Bible till you send for the doctor in your last illness, and then find the Bible a sealed book, and dark as the cloud between the hosts of Israel and Egypt, to your anxious soul! Beware lest you go on saying all your life, "Men do very well without all this Bible-reading," and find at length, to your cost, that men do very ill, and end in hell! Beware lest the day come, when you will feel, "Had I but honoured the Bible as much as I have honoured the newspaper, I should not have been left without comfort in my last hour!" Bible-neglecting reader, I give you a plain warning. The plague-cross is at present on your door. The Lord have mercy upon your soul![1]

(2) These pages may fall into the hands of someone who is

---

[1] During the Great Plague of London (1665), infected victims were boarded up in their homes; the door was then marked with a red cross and the words "Lord have mercy on us" were inscribed on it. Death was imminent, usually within four days.

willing to begin reading the Bible, but wants advice on the subject. Reader, are you that man? Listen to me, and I will give you a few short hints.

(*a*) For one thing, *begin reading your Bible this very day*. The way to do a thing is to do it, and the way to read the Bible is actually to read it. It is not meaning, or wishing, or resolving, or intending, or thinking about it, which will advance you one step. You must positively read. There is no royal road in this matter, any more than in the matter of prayer. If you cannot read yourself, you must persuade somebody else to read to you. But one way or another, through eyes or ears, the words of Scripture must actually pass before your mind.

(*b*) For another thing, *read the Bible with an earnest desire to understand it*. Think not for a moment that the great object is to turn over a certain quantity of printed paper, and that it matters nothing whether you understand it or not. Some ignorant people seem to fancy that all is done if they clear off so many chapters every day, though they may not have a notion what they are all about, and only know that they have pushed on their mark so many leaves. This is turning Bible-reading into a mere form. It is almost as bad as the Popish habit of buying indulgences by saying an almost fabulous number of *Ave Marias* and Paternosters. It reminds one of the poor Hottentot[1] who ate up a Dutch hymn-book because he saw it comforted his neighbours' hearts. Settle it down in your mind, as a general principle, that a Bible not understood is a Bible that does no good. Say to yourself often as you read, "What is all this about?" Dig for the meaning like a man digging for Australian gold. Work hard, and do not give up the work in a hurry.

(*c*) For another thing, *read the Bible with deep reverence*. Say to your soul, whenever you open the Bible, "O my soul, thou art going to read a message from God." The sentences of judges and the speeches of kings are received with awe and respect. How much more reverence is due to the words of the Judge of judges and King of kings! Avoid, as you would cursing and swearing, that irreverent habit of mind, into which some modern divines have unhappily fallen, in speaking about the Bible. They handle

---

[1] The Khoikhoi, a nomadic people who inhabited southern & western South Africa when the region was colonized in the seventeenth century.

the contents of the holy book as carelessly and disrespectfully as if the writers were such men as themselves. They make one think of a child composing a book to expose the fancied ignorance of his own father, or of a pardoned murderer criticising the handwriting and style of his own reprieve, or of a man botanising on his mother's grave. Enter rather into the spirit of the words spoken to Moses on Mount Horeb: "Put thy shoes from off thy feet; the place whereon thou standest is holy ground." (Exod. 3:5.)

(*d*) For another thing, *read the Bible with earnest prayer for the teaching and help of the Holy Spirit*. Here is the rock on which many make shipwreck at the very outset. They do not ask for wisdom and instruction, and so they find the Bible dark, and carry nothing away from it. You should pray for the Spirit to guide you into all truth. You should beg the Lord Jesus Christ to "open your understanding," as He did that of His disciples. (Luke 24:45.) The Lord God, by whose inspiration the book was written, keeps the keys of the book, and alone can enable you to understand it profitably. Nine times over in one psalm does David cry, "Teach me." Five times over in the same psalm does he say, "Give me understanding." (Ps. 119.) Well says John Owen, Dean of Christ Church, Oxford, "There is a sacred light in the Word: but there is a covering and veil on the eyes of men, so that they cannot behold it aright. Now the removal of this veil is the peculiar work of the Holy Spirit." Humble prayer will throw more light on your Bible than Poole's *Synopsis*, or all the commentaries that were ever written. Remember this, and say always, "O God, for Christ's sake, give me the teaching of the Spirit."

(*e*) For another thing, *read the Bible with childlike faith and humility*. Open your heart as you open your book, and say, "Speak, Lord, for Thy servant heareth." (1 Sam. 3:9, 10.) Resolve to believe implicitly whatever you find there, however much it may run counter to your own prejudices. Resolve to receive heartily every statement of truth, whether you like it or not. Beware of that miserable habit of mind into which some readers of the Bible fall. They receive some doctrines, because they like them. They reject others, because they are condemning to themselves, or to some lover, or relation, or friend. At this rate the Bible is useless. Are we to be judges of what ought to be in the Word? Do we know better than God? Settle it down in your mind that you will receive all, and believe all, and that what you cannot understand you will take on trust. Remember, when you pray, you are speaking to God, and God hears you. But, remember, when you read, God is speaking to you, and you are not to "answer again," but to listen. (Titus 2:9.)

(*f*) For another thing, *read the Bible in a spirit of obedience and self-application*. Sit down to the study of it with a daily determination that *you* will live by its rules, rest on its statements, and act on its commands. Consider, as you travel through every chapter, "How does this affect *my* position and course of conduct? What does this teach *me?*" It is poor work to read the Bible for mere curiosity and speculative purposes, in order to fill your head and store your mind with opinions, while you do not allow the book to influence your heart and life. That Bible is read best, which is practised most.

(*g*) For another thing, *read the Bible daily*. Make it a part of every day's business to read and meditate on some portion of God's Word. Private means of grace are just as needful every day for our souls, as food and clothing are for our bodies. Yesterday's bread will not feed the labourer today, and today's bread will not feed the labourer tomorrow. Do as the Israelites did in the wilderness. Gather your manna fresh every morning. Choose your own seasons and hours. Do not scramble over and hurry your reading. Give your Bible the best, and not the worst, part of your time. But whatever plan you pursue, let it be a rule of your life to visit the throne of grace and the Bible every day.

(*h*) For another thing, *read all the Bible, and read it in an orderly way*. I fear there are many parts of the Word which some people never read at all. This is, to say the least, a very presumptuous habit. "All Scripture is profitable." (2 Tim. 3:16.) To this habit may be traced the want of broad, well-proportioned views of truth, which is so common in this day. Some people's Bible-reading is a system of perpetual dipping and picking. They do not seem to have an idea of regularly going through the whole book. This also is a great mistake. No doubt in times of sickness and affliction it is allowable to search out seasonable portions. But with this exception, I believe it is by far the best plan to begin the Old and New Testaments at the same time, read each straight through to the end, and then begin again. This is a matter in which every one must be persuaded in his own mind. I can only say it has been my own plan for forty years, and I have never seen cause to alter it.

(*i*) For another thing, *read the Bible fairly and honestly*. Determine to take everything in its plain, obvious meaning, and regard all forced interpretations with great suspicion. As a general rule, whatever a verse of the Bible seems to mean, it does mean. Cecil's rule is a very valuable one—"The right way of interpreting Scripture is to take it as we find it, without any attempt to force it into any particular system." Well said Hooker, "I hold it for a most infallible rule in the exposition of Scripture that when a literal construction will stand, the furthest from the literal is commonly the worst."[1]

(*j*) In the last place, *read the Bible with Christ continually in view*. The grand primary object of all Scripture is to testify of Jesus. Old Testament ceremonies are shadows of Christ. Old Testament judges and deliverers are types of Christ. Old Testament history shows the world's need of Christ. Old Testament prophecies are full of Christ's sufferings, and of Christ's glory yet to come. The first advent and the second, the Lord's humiliation and the Lord's kingdom, the cross and the crown, shine forth everywhere in the Bible. Keep fast hold on this clue, if you would read the Bible aright.

Reader, I might easily add to these hints, if time permitted. Few and short as they are, you will find them worth attention. Act upon them, and I firmly believe you will never be allowed to miss the way to heaven. Act upon them, and you will find light continually increasing in your mind. No book of evidence can be compared with that internal evidence which he obtains, who daily uses the Word in the right way. Such a man does not need the books of learned men, like Paley, and Wilson, and M'Ilvaine.[2] He has the witness in himself. The book satisfies and feeds his soul. A poor Christian woman once said to an infidel, "I am no scholar. I cannot argue like you. But I know that honey is honey, because it leaves a sweet taste in my mouth. And I know the Bible to be God's book, because of the taste it leaves in my heart."

---

[1] Richard Hooker (*c*. 1554–1600).

[2] William Paley (1743–1805), Daniel Wilson (1778–1858), and Charles M'Ilvaine (1799–1873) were apologists for the Christian faith.

(3) These pages may fall into the hands of someone who *loves and believes the Bible, and yet reads it but little*. I fear there are many such in this day. It is a day of bustle and hurry. It is a day of talking, and committee meetings, and public work. These things are all very well in their way, but I fear that sometimes they clip and cut short the private reading of the Bible. Reader, does your conscience tell you that you are one of the persons I speak of? Listen to me, and I will say a few things which deserve your serious attention.

You are the man that is likely to *get little comfort from the Bible in time of need*. Trial is a sifting season. Affliction is a searching wind, which strips the leaves off the trees, and brings to light the birds' nests. Now I fear that your stores of Bible consolations may one day run very low. I fear lest you should find yourself at last on very short allowance, and come into harbour weak, worn, and thin.

You are the man that is likely *never to be established in the truth*. I shall not be surprised to hear that you are troubled with doubts and questionings about assurance, grace, faith, perseverance, and the like. The devil is an old and cunning enemy. Like the Benjamites, he can "throw stones at a hair breadth, and not miss." (Judg. 20:16.) He can quote Scripture readily enough, when he pleases. Now you are not sufficiently ready with your weapons to be able to fight a good fight with him. Your armour does not fit you well. Your sword sits loosely in your hand.

You are the man that is likely to *make mistakes in life*. I shall not wonder if I am told that you have erred about your own marriage, erred about your children's education, erred about the conduct of your household, erred about the company you keep. The world you steer through is full of rocks, and shoals, and sandbanks. You are not sufficiently familiar either with the lights or charts.

You are the man that is likely to *be carried away by some specious false teacher for a season*. It will not surprise me if I hear that some one of those clever, eloquent men, who can "make the worse appear the better cause,"[1] is leading you into many follies. You are wanting in ballast. No wonder if you are tossed to and fro, like a cork on the waves.

---

[1] John Milton (1608-1674), *Paradise Lost* (1667).

Reader, all these are uncomfortable things. I want you to escape them all. Take the advice I offer you this day. Do not merely read your Bible "a little," but read it a great deal. "Let the word of Christ dwell in you richly." (Col. 3:16.) Do not be a mere babe in spiritual knowledge. Seek to become "well-instructed in the kingdom of heaven," and to be continually adding new things to old. (Matt. 13:52.) A religion of feeling is an uncertain thing. It is like the tide, sometimes high, and sometimes low. It is like the moon, sometimes bright, and sometimes dim. A religion of deep Bible-knowledge is a firm and lasting possession. It enables a man not merely to say, "I feel hope in Christ," but "I know whom I have believed." (2 Tim. 1:12.)

(4) These pages may fall into the hands of someone who *reads the Bible much, and yet fancies he is no better for his reading.* This is a crafty temptation of the devil. At one stage he says, "Do not read the Bible at all." At another he says, "Your reading does you no good: give it up." Reader, are you that man? I feel for you from the bottom of my soul. Let me try to do you good.

Do not think you are getting no good from the Bible, merely because you do not see that good day by day. The greatest effects are by no means those which make the most noise, and are most easily observed. The greatest effects are often silent, quiet, and hard to detect at the time they are being produced. Think of the influence of the Moon upon the Earth, and of the air upon the human lungs. Remember how silently the dew falls, and how imperceptibly the grass grows. There may be far more doing than you think in your soul by your Bible-reading.

The Word may be gradually producing deep *impressions* on your heart, of which you are not at present aware. Often when the memory is retaining no facts, the character of a man is receiving some everlasting impression. Is sin becoming every year more hateful to you? Is Christ becoming every year more precious? Is holiness becoming every year more lovely and desirable in your eyes? If these things are so, take courage. The Bible is doing you good, though you may not be able to trace it out day by day.

The Bible may be restraining you from some sin or delusion, into which you would otherwise run. It may be daily keeping you back, and hedging you up, and preventing many a false step. Ah! reader, you might soon find this out to your cost, if you were to cease reading the Word. The very familiarity of blessings sometimes makes us insensible to their value. Resist the devil. Settle it down in your mind as an established rule that, whether you feel it at the moment or not, you are inhaling spiritual health by reading the Bible, and insensibly becoming more strong.

(5) There may be some into whose hands these pages will fall who *really love the Bible, live upon the Bible, and read it much*. Reader, are you one of these? Give me your attention, and I will mention a few things which we shall do well to lay to heart for time to come.

Let us resolve to *read the Bible more and more* every year we live. Let us try to get it rooted in our memories, and engrafted into our hearts. Let us be thoroughly well provisioned with it against the voyage of death. Who knows but we may have a very stormy passage? Sight and hearing may fail us, and we may be in deep waters. Oh, to have the Word "hid in our hearts" in such an hour as that! (Ps. 119:11.)

Let us resolve to be *more watchful over our Bible-reading* every year that we live. Let us be jealously careful about the time we give to it, and the manner that time is spent. Let us beware of omitting our daily reading without sufficient cause. Let us not be gaping, and yawning, and dozing over our book while we read. Let us read like a London merchant studying the City article in the *Times*, or like a wife reading a husband's letter from a distant land. Let us be very careful that we never exalt any minister, or sermon, or book, or tract, or friend, above the Word. Cursed be that book, or tract, or human counsel which creeps in between us and the Bible, and hides the Bible from our eyes! Once more I say, let us be very watchful. The moment we open the Bible, the devil sits down by our side to tempt us. Oh! to read with a hungry spirit, and a simple desire for edification!

Let us resolve to *honour the Bible more in our families*. Let us read it morning and evening to our children and households, and not be ashamed to let men see that we do so. Let us not be discouraged by seeing no good arise from it. The Bible-reading in a family has kept many a one from the gaol, the workhouse, and the *Gazette*, if it has not kept him from hell.

Let us resolve to *meditate more on the Bible*. It is good to take with us two or three texts, when we go out into the world, and to turn them over in our minds, whenever we have a little leisure. It keeps out many vain thoughts. It clenches the nail of daily reading. It preserves our souls from stagnating, and breeding corrupt things. It sanctifies and quickens our memories, and prevents their becoming like those ponds where the frogs live, but the fish die.

Let us resolve to *talk more to believers about the Bible* when we meet them. Alas! the conversation of Christians, when they do meet, is often sadly unprofitable. How many frivolous, and trifling, and uncharitable things are said! Let us bring out the Bible more, and it will help to drive the devil away, and keep our hearts in tune. Oh! that we may all strive so to walk together in this evil world that Jesus may often draw near and go with us, as He went with the two disciples journeying to Emmaus!

Let us resolve to *prize the Bible more*. Let us not fear being idolaters of this blessed book. Men may easily make an idol of the Church, of ministers, of sacraments, or of intellect. Men cannot make an idol of the Word. Let us regard all who would damage the authority of the Bible, or impugn its credit, as spiritual robbers. We are travelling through a wilderness: they rob us of our only guide. We are voyaging over a stormy sea: they rob us of our only compass. We are toiling over a weary road: they pluck our staff out of our hands. And what do these spiritual robbers give us in place of the Bible? What do they offer as a guide and provision for our souls? Nothing! absolutely nothing! Big swelling words! Empty promises of new light! High-sounding jargon, but nothing substantial and real. They would fain take from us the bread of life, and they do not give us in its place so much as a stone. Let us turn a deaf ear to them. Let us firmly grasp and prize the Bible more and more, the more it is assaulted.

Let us resolve to *remember those who have not got the Bible*. Let us labour to raise them from their low estate. None are so poor as those who have not the Scriptures. Let us think of them with pity and compassion, and not judge them by the standard of people who have the Word.

Let us deal gently with our Irish brother. He may do many things which fill us with horror. But he "errs, not knowing the Scriptures." (Matt. 22:29.) *He has no Bible.*

Let us judge charitably our Italian brother. He may seem

superstitious, and lazy, and indolent, and incapable of anything great or good. But he "errs, not knowing the Scriptures." *He has no Bible.*

Let us think lovingly of all Roman Catholic laymen on the Continent. We may feel disgusted by their adoring the Holy Coat of Tréves.[1] We may be shocked at their credulity about the Winking Picture of the Virgin at Rimini.[2] But we must remember that men will eat mice and rats in time of famine, and we must not marvel if souls feed on trash and garbage when priests debar them from reading the Word. They "err, not knowing the Scriptures." *They have no Bibles.*

Last of all, let us resolve to *live by the Bible more and more* every year we live. Let us resolutely take account of all our opinions and practices, of our habits and tempers, of our behaviour in public and in private, in the world, and by our own firesides. Let us measure all by the Bible, and resolve, by God's help, to conform to it. Oh! that we may learn increasingly to "cleanse our ways" by the Word! (Ps. 119:9.)

Reader, I commend all these things to your serious and prayerful attention. I want the ministers of my beloved country to be Bible-reading ministers; the congregations, Bible-reading congregations; and the nation, a Bible-reading nation. To bring about this desirable end, I cast my mite into God's treasury. The Lord grant that in your case it may prove not to have been in vain!

I remain, your affectionate friend,

J.C. RYLE.

---

[1] A seamless garb which, according to legend, belonged to the newborn Jesus and retained a miraculous capacity to grow. Though the Bible says nothing of it, and no record of it exists prior to the twelfth century, it eventually became an object of adoration. Since the sixteenth century, popes have paid it tribute, masses said in its honour, pilgrimages declared on its behalf, and indulgences proclaimed for those who would venerate it.

[2] A picture of Mary that was given to a church at Rimini, Italy, in 1810, and believed to have winked in 1850.

Beneath the sands of time lie the ashes of saints who were burnt alive for the Protestant freedoms we now enjoy. Written to our "children's children," *Light From Old Times* extols the faith—in life and in death—of those who delivered the English-speaking gospel to us. Hardcover, volume I of the collected works, 430 Smythe-sewn pages, ISBN 0-9677603-0-5.

Picking up where *Light* left off, *Christian Leaders* sketches the lives and ministries of those who preached the gospel during the eighteenth-century revival. George Whitefield, John Wesley, Henry Venn, Daniel Rowlands, Augustus Toplady, and others are profiled in these pages. Hardcover, vol. II of the collected works, 420 Smythe-sewn pages, ISBN 0-9677603-7-2.

www.charlesnolanpublishers.com

J.C. Ryle once said, "If you want to heat a church, put a stove in the pulpit," and judging from these sermons he knew whereof he spake. Arranged shortly before his death, *The Christian Race* is a fitting tribute to Ryle's 60-year ministry, showing that his furnace still burns hot. Vol. III of the collected works, 300 Smythe-sewn pages, ISBN 0-9677603-8-0.

Protestant and evangelical, *Knots Untied* is considered by many to be J.C. Ryle's *magnum opus*. He wrote, "Let us have clear systematic views of the gospel of the grace of God. Nothing else will do in the hour of sickness, in the day of trial, on the bed of death, and in the swellings of Jordan." Hardcover, vol. IV, 444 Smythe-sewn pages, ISBN 0-9677603-2-1.

www.charlesnolanpublishers.com

Part of the nineteenth-century "Little Gem" series, *Shall We Know One Another & Other Papers* is a wonderful collection of essays, replete with rare nuggets, goodly stones, and pearls of wisdom from J.C. Ryle's treasure chest. "I am very jealous for my Master's cause. Anything, anything, to make it more lovely before man!" Booklet, 68 pages, ISBN 0-9677603-6-4.

Thoughts for Young Men should be mandatory reading for men of all ages and stations in life—young, old, bond or free: "If I can only say something to keep some young man in the right way, and preserve him from faults and sins, which may mar his prospects both for time and eternity, I shall be very thankful." Booklet, 68 pages, ISBN 0-9677603-9-9.

www.charlesnolanpublishers.com

Some books defy description, and *Holiness* no doubt is one of them. This work is quite simply magnificent. John MacArthur says, "In any list of must-read books, *Holiness* should be somewhere near the very top." Foreword by Martyn Lloyd-Jones, volume VII of Ryle's collected works, 440 Smythe-sewn pages, ISBN 0-9677603-4-8 (hardcover), 0-9677603-5-6 (pb).

"*A Call to Prayer* is J.C. Ryle's clarion wake-up call about prayer. I commend it as a potent remedy for spiritual apathy and weak Christianity. If you heed Bishop Ryle's advice, your walk with the Lord will be energized by an infusion of vitality and spiritual power you never imagined possible." — John MacArthur. Booklet, 36 pages, ISBN 0-9722374-0-2.

www.charlesnolanpublishers.com

"How Readest Thou?"
by
J.C. Ryle

Set in
10.5 on 12.6 Adobe Jenson
on
60# Husky Offset
Composed at
Ruptüred Disc Studios, Moscow
Printed & bound by
Jostens Printing & Publishing
Cover design by
CAROLUS MAGNUS